THE
RED ARROWS

THE
RED ARROWS
REDS, ROLLING, NOW!

PHOTOGRAPHED BY
RICHARD COOKE
WRITTEN BY
GILLIAN COOKE

PLANET BOOKS
Published by
W.H. Allen & Co Plc
London

Text © Gillian Cooke, 1987
Photographs © Richard Cooke, 1987
This edition © W.H. Allen & Co Plc, 1987
Appendix © British Aerospace Plc, 1985

First published in 1987 by Planet Books, a division
of W.H. Allen & Co Plc
Reprinted November 1987, January 1988

Set by Phoenix Photosetting, Chatham, Kent
Printed and bound in Barcelona, Spain by Cronion, S.A.
for the Publishers W.H. Allen & Co Plc,
44 Hill Street, London W1X 8LB

Designed by Peter Laws

British Library Cataloguing in Publication Data

Cooke, Richard
    The Red Arrows.
    1. Great Britain. *Royal Air Force.*
    Aerobatic Team
    I. Title   II. Cooke, Gillian
    797.5′4′0941   UG635.G7

    ISBN 1 85227 010 1

The appendix to this book has been reproduced by
courtesy of British Aerospace PLC and with their
consent and is the copyright of British Aerospace
PLC.

Front cover picture: The Red Arrows flying a special
sortie for the BBC Television series, *The Moment of
Truth*

Back cover picture: Flight Lieutenant Charlie
McIlroy, Synchro Lead in 1987, prepares to strap in

Frontispiece: The Red Arrows' trademark – a perfect
Diamond Nine

CONTENTS

ACKNOWLEDGEMENTS

A book about the Red Arrows could not exist without the cooperation of both past and present members of the Team, and we would like to take this opportunity to thank them all for their help. We would particularly like to thank Squadron Leader Alan Voyle, the Senior Engineering Officer from 1975 to 1979, who gave a great deal of technical assistance during the development of rear-facing photography. Special thanks must also go to the 1986 Team, the engineers John Chantry and Frank Lovejoy, all the ground crew, the Manager Henry Ploszek and his staff, and in particular the Leader, Squadron Leader Richard Thomas. They all gave up a great deal of time and were extremely hospitable, both during a very busy display season and the following winter training.

Thanks are also due to Heather Thomas, Anne Ploszek and the rest of the wives, to Air Commodore A. B. Blackley and Wing Commander Charles Boyack who welcomed us on to the station, to John Godden of British Aerospace and to Pat Hornsey of W.H. Allen who responded to a photograph which landed on her desk one day and began the whole project.

Finally we should thank our children, James and Lucy, who put up with our constant absence during the summer months.

Previous page: Looping in Concorde formation

For James and Lucy

CHAPTER ONE
INTRODUCING
THE RED ARROWS

A sk any man in any street to name an aerobatic display team and he will probably say "The Red Arrows". Many different teams, both civil and military, appear at air shows all over the world but most would acknowledge that the Red Arrows are the cream. Since 1965 they have looped, dived and rolled their way through hundreds of displays and many thousands of flying hours, but even people who see them time and time again are still thrilled by their aerobatic expertise.

The skills displayed by the Red Arrows have their roots right back in the history of the Royal Air Force and the Royal Flying Corps. As long ago as the First World War of 1914–18, when pilots had to use all their aircraft's capabilities to avoid enemy attack, aerobatics were an important part of their training. Formation flying was also vital to bring maximum fire power safely to a target in the shortest possible time. Combining the two skills was soon recognised as a most spectacular way of catching the imagination of potential new recruits, and instructors from the Central Flying School (CFS), using a succession of different training aircraft, demonstrated formation aerobatics at RAF flying pageants throughout the 1920s and 1930s.

During the Second World War from 1939–45, however, the public's interest switched to the more powerful fighter aircraft that had come into service, and in 1947 the first RAF jet formation aerobatic team of three Vampires was formed. Although CFS resumed its tradition of flying aerobatic teams in 1952 using Meteor T.7s, until 1963 the RAF's official teams were all drawn from

Above and right: Hawker Siddeley Gnats formed the first Red Arrows Aerobatic Team in 1965. They flew over 1,200 displays before being replaced by the new British Aerospace Hawk in 1980

the latest fighter squadrons. Each year a different one was picked and the best remembered is probably No. 111 ("Treble One") Squadron's team of sixteen black-painted Hunters, The Black Arrows, which was formed in 1957. The team established a world record at Farnborough in 1958 when, supplemented by six borrowed aircraft, they looped twenty-two Hunters in a single formation.

The last aerobatic team from an operational squadron was the Firebirds, which flew nine fast and powerful Lightnings from No. 56 Squadron. They were formed in 1963 but by this time it had already become clear that it was simply not cost-effective to withdraw a squadron from front-line duties for a season of display flying. It was decided that in future all formation teams must be drawn from training units and the CFS, with its long tradition of aerobatic flying, was the obvious choice. In 1958 a team of Jet Provosts from CFS, known first as the Pelicans and then as the Red Pelicans, had been formed and in 1964 they became the RAF's official display team.

Unfortunately the Jet Provost, though a fairly easy aircraft to fly, was not spectacular to watch. The air-show crowds had become used to the dramatic sight of the black Hunters and the tremendous power of the Lightnings, and it soon became clear that Jet Provosts would not fill the gap. The main roles of the team were to inspire potential recruits and to demonstrate the versatility of the aircraft and the skills of the pilots, but the Jet Provosts could not generate the same excitement as the earlier teams. It was decided to form a team from the instructors at No. 4 Flying Training Unit at RAF Valley on Anglesey, using the RAF's new Gnat trainers.

The first public appearance of the Yellowjacks, so called because of their yellow paint scheme, was at Royal Naval Air Station Culdrose on 25th July, 1964. They were so successful that in 1965 a permanent Gnat display team was formed. The new team, led by Flight Lieutenant Lee Jones, the leader of the Yellowjacks and an ex-member of the Black Arrows, was called the Red Arrows. The colour red had long been associated with the Central

Flying School's formation teams and the shape of the new Gnat trainer lent itself to the name "Arrows", as well as retaining a link with the famous Black Arrows. There is also a story that the colour might have been chosen because the RAF already possessed large quantities of red, white and blue paint for painting roundels. Blue would not show up against the sky, white would need continual cleaning, so red was the ideal choice.

Brian Nice, then a young Flight Lieutenant, was in the Red Arrows for that first season. He had been flying with the Red Pelicans for two years and, along with other pilots from the Pelicans and the Yellowjacks, he became part of the new Royal Air Force Aerobatic Team. In those early days the pilots, conscious of being the first permanent display team, felt they had to establish themselves. They were worried about whether the Gnat would be right for the display and a lot of the manoeuvres were being tried out for the first time ever using swept wing aircraft. There was a great deal of innovation and experimentation and they hoped that on the day the manoeuvres would work. Throughout the first season the display was improvised as they tried to arrive at the right mix of formations – ones which were safe and which the public would like.

Compared with today's Aerobatic Team, the Red Arrows of 1965 were far less professionally organised. They did not have the administrative back-up that they have now and were, as Brian Nice says, "a little more carefree". At that stage the idea of a permanent team was on trial and no-one knew for certain if the Team would carry on.

Brian Nice looks back on his time in the Team as something very special.

"It was absolutely unique, a time that will never ever happen again. Being in the Arrows is not being in the RAF. I think anybody will tell you that. You live apart from the Air Force. You have a different routine and you do feel in a sense isolated from it. You are glad of the technical support but the nature of receptions, crowds, living in hotels and being away for long periods, makes it hard to identify with the rest of the Air Force. You are a very tight-knit team and it is very hard to go back to a more ordinary life after it. You do know it's going to end though, and you make the best of the years you have with the Team. You do have to adapt to leaving and say 'Thank God I was that lucky and that privileged to have had that time.' You very quickly reconcile yourself to the fact that life cannot be lived at that level of adrenalin, with being in the public eye and the constant challenge. You have to be philosophical about it.

"We were a new team with new aircraft and when we flew in Europe we were compared to all the other display teams there. The country's reputation was at stake and we were very much aware of that. Someone said to me – in fact, I heard this many times in Europe – this is the best advertisement not just for the Air Force, but for your country.

"You do more for Britain than a hundred ambassadors and high level visits by MPs. There is no way you can put a value on that. You are very aware of it when you taxi out. I know we were very aware of people thinking 'Ah England, we'll see how they do.' At a time when our international reputation was not that good, there was a lot riding on us, especially with the other display teams there.

"Each Team member is an individual of course. You come together hoping you can make a team. When you are up in the air you have to have total, implicit trust in each other. When you slide back the other guys will move, when you go into cloud or turbulence comes you know how you will each react. That trust, you feel it in the air. Sometimes a show goes beautifully and it is smooth and lovely, another time there are cross winds and you are up and down. You have to believe in each other otherwise you could not do it."

At the beginning the Red Arrows were based, on permanent detachment, at RAF Fairford in Gloucestershire, The Yellowjacks had been using five aircraft with five spare but the Red Arrows soon increased the display to seven. The first public display of the new Red Arrows was at Biggin Hill in May 1965. They were an immediate success and by the end of that year they had flown sixty-five

displays in Britain, France, Italy, Holland, Belgium and Germany.

In 1966 Squadron Leader Ray Hanna took over as Leader. Two spare pilots were established and the Team continued to fly seven aircraft on display. It soon became obvious that carrying spare pilots was not a good idea. The display was so specialised that each position had its own specific demands and required a great deal of practice to perfect. Any pilot capable of flying each position would need more training and probably more skill than any one member of the Team. He would, naturally enough, not be satisfied with being a reserve. In 1967 the Team flew with only seven pilots, but then in 1968 a team of nine aircraft was approved. From that time the Red Arrows' classic "Diamond 9" formation became their trademark.

For the first four years the Team operated as a detachment from CFS, but in 1969 the unit was established permanently as a standard RAF squadron. Each year as Team members completed their tours of duty, new pilots joined the Team and over the years the aircraft also underwent some changes. The original red tail fins were repainted in red, white and blue, and by 1967 the white lightning line had been added to the side of the fuselage in front of the engine air intakes. The biggest change came in 1979. By this time the Red Arrows squadron was based at RAF Kemble in Gloucestershire. They had used the Hawker Siddeley Gnat for fifteen very successful years and had flown 1,292 performances in eighteen different countries. By 1979, however, the British Aerospace Hawk had replaced the Gnat as the RAF's standard advanced jet trainer, and the Red Arrows, as a flagship for the modern service, had to accommodate this change. They took delivery of the Hawk trainer in the winter of 1979/80 and the pilots converted to the new aeroplane. With a great deal of hard work from both the pilots and the ground crew the new display was ready in time for the start of the 1980 season. The Red Arrows are now based at RAF Scampton in Lincolnshire, and it is from here that they fly each season to display to the public, both in Britain and abroad.

CHAPTER TWO
BEFORE THE SHOW

The public face of the Red Arrows is seen all round the country from April to September each year. They are a high spot of any air show and the organisers know that if they can persuade the Team to come, the success of their show is guaranteed. What the spectators may not realise is the amount of time and planning required to enable the Red Arrows to appear at all.

The man who is largely responsible for this organisation is the Team Manager. He works very closely with the Team and in particular the Team Leader and travels with them to all the displays. He flies the tenth Hawk, the "Spare", and is the man the spectators hear giving the commentary. He is not, as some think, a spare pilot but has a very important and quite separate job. Helped by a Warrant Officer Adjutant, a corporal and two Senior Aircraftmen (SACs), he deals with most of the organisation and paperwork involved in planning the Team's appearances.

Warrant Officer George Thorne, who was the Team Adjutant from 1975 to 1983, worked closely with the Red Arrows' Managers during that period. He helped liaise with display organisers, arrange hotel bookings and cope with all the problems that arise with taking ten jets, ten pilots and about thirty ground crew around the country.

He greatly enjoyed his years working with the Team and successive Managers but says wryly, "It's the old, old story. Whatever you do in life, if you have been there a long time, you tell the new chap how it all works and within a week he's telling you how to do it!

Above: The Red Arrows' Hawks on a high-level transit to display in Europe

Right: The Team Manager, Squadron Leader Henry Ploszek, is sometimes flown to the commentary position at a display site in a Gazelle helicopter from RAF Shawbury

"The first time I ever heard of the Red Arrows was in 1966 when I was stationed at RAF Wattisham. One of my sons asked if we could go to Bentwaters to see the Red Arrows. I though it must be some kind of Red Indian show. I didn't realise that Bentwaters was an air base but I wasn't going to tell *him* that! At that time I didn't like air shows and wasn't too impressed with the other teams but then they handed over to the Red Arrows commentator and as they began their display I thought, this is better, this could be interesting.

"When I first joined the squadron I wasn't intending to stay long. In the beginning I didn't go away with them, but then one year I was allowed to go to Jersey. I enjoyed that and so I stayed and stayed. Soon after that I went with the Team to an air display in France. The French view an air show like a picnic. They get out their table-cloths and sit down with their food, looking up occasionally as the aeroplanes fly over. Then the Red Arrows began their display and I had never seen Frenchmen leave their food before. They all got up, watched and applauded.

"The Red Arrows didn't display in France very often because of their strict regulations about flying over the spectators. There are a few occasions, like the arrival, when they do fly over the crowd, and the show wouldn't be the same without it. The French won't allow that and the Team Leader used to have to sign a certificate saying that he would comply with the regulations.

"As the years went by I began putting my name down on the Operation Orders and no-one seemed to mind – except the wife. I didn't bother to go to the boring places but I went all over Europe, on the Middle East tour and to the United States. I was in charge of imprest – the money advanced to the men to pay their expenses – and it got quite complicated on the Middle East tour with so many different countries and different currencies.

"During that tour, when we were in Bahrain, we nearly lost one of the pilots! We had been out one evening and he had got separated and couldn't remember the name of the hotel. He spent two and an half hours in the back of a taxi going round the city trying to find the rest of the Team. At each hotel the taxi driver had gone in and asked: 'Have you got Red Arrow?' If the pilot hadn't eventually seen me outside the entrance to our hotel, I think he might still be there.

"The organisation behind the trips was always so complicated, I often had nightmares wondering what would happen if it didn't work. In fact, the only time I do remember something failing to turn up was in the days of the Gnat. The aeroplane took liquid oxygen and it became very difficult to get. One weekend we were going to the United States Air Force Base at Ramstein in West Germany. We had asked them to provide liquid oxygen for the pilots which they said would be no problem. When we turned up it wasn't there and there was no way the Americans could get it. In the end the Team had to transit low-level to RAF Wildenrath which luckily wasn't far away."

Squadron Leader Henry Ploszek joined the Team as Manager in 1984. In the 1960s he had flown with the Lightning aerobatic team, the Firebirds, but he was not sure if the Red Arrows' Manager's job would suit him.

"The Team normally choose who they want. There are always lots of people wanting to volunteer for this job but it's such a tightly-knit unit that you have got to get on with the whole Team. I was Squadron Leader Operations in Cyprus before this so I got to know them very well when they came out for their winter work-ups. When their Manager was due to leave, they asked me to do the job. At first I was not at all keen. I thought I was too old. The Managers are usually young Squadron Leaders, but the Team kept asking me and I decided to do it. I enjoy the challenge of moving around and I feel about ten years younger now!"

The Manager is the man most closely connected to the Team, and spectators at air shows are more likely to catch sight of him than they are of the pilots. When he gives the commentary from the display site, Squadron Leader Ploszek's red flying suit and silver head of hair make him very easy to spot – the hair has, apparently, been that colour for years, not just since he took over the job.

The planning that goes into each display begins before the end of the previous season. This is when the organisers for the next year's shows write to the RAF's Participation Committee in the Ministry of Defence. This committee will decide how the RAF can take part in air shows, carnivals and fêtes around the country and abroad. It deals not only with the Red Arrows but with all the RAF displays for that year, including the Falcons parachute display team, and solo display aircraft like the Harrier, the Tornado and the Hawk.

Many of the organisers are experts. They know the places the Red Arrows are likely to appear, and they know that if they hold their show on a date which ties in with another major air display reasonably nearby, there is a strong possibility that the Team will be able to visit them too. New air shows with inexperienced organisers sometimes take a couple of years to learn the ropes and, in picking an arbitrary date for their show, miss the chance of a Red Arrows display. The prestigious regular events like Biggin Hill and Farnborough are always guaranteed a visit from the Team but small villages with experience, like Lochinver in Scotland, also have a good chance. They have learnt over the years that if they tag on to a Lossiemouth show, the Red Arrows may be able to display for them during the same weekend.

By late September the list of requests lands on the desks of the Team Leader and Team Manager at RAF Scampton. They will look through it and discuss the venues that look feasible. "Some places drop out automatically," says Squadron Leader Ploszek. "If there are two or three important shows in one part of the country and also one at the other end of Britain on the same weekend, the Team would not have the time or the fuel to cover them all and the odd one would have to drop out. However, we do bear that in mind, and if it has happened for a couple of years, we make a special effort and tell the Participation Committee. We try and spread ourselves around the country as much as possible."

The shows are each given gradings which reflect their value to recruiting and public relations.

The recruiters will decide which shows are the most important for them and grade them A, B, C or D accordingly; and the public relations office, looking from their point of view, will do the same. A combination of AA means the Red Arrows are bound to appear, but a CC would have to be very lucky. Sometimes the grades are a complete contrast. There may be few recruiting possibilities in a particular area, but the public relations exercise is still important. Lochinver, for example, is only a small village but the inhabitants put up with a lot of aircraft noise during the year. A display from the Red Arrows across their tiny harbour during the summer, when the area is packed with holiday-makers, is one way the RAF can thank the villagers for their forebearance.

When the Team Leader and Team Manager have discussed which displays seem possible, the list goes back to the Participation Committee. The committee meets in November and consists of an Air Commodore, a civil servant secretary, two under secretaries and representatives from all the RAF display teams and from each RAF command that has display aircraft.

The Air Commodore will go through his list and say where he thinks the RAF can appear and which display teams it can send. It will take two or three hours as members of the committee add their comments and ideas. Once the Participation Committee has discussed the list, it goes up to the Air Board which gives the final approval. This then becomes the RAF's participation around the country for that year. In 1986 it cost each show £2,070 plus VAT and £550 insurance to have the Red Arrows – it cost the RAF a lot more than that in fuel alone.

Once the list has been approved, the Participation Committee will then write to the organisers, to tell them what the RAF can provide for their show. As soon as the letters have been received, the Red Arrows can begin their organisation.

The Team Adjutant will send each organiser a form to fill in. It tells them how the Team will operate and what they will need, and also asks detailed questions relating to the operational side of

Above: The pilots and ground crew strap in for a
transit flight to the next display site

Right: Late afternoon practice

the display. The Red Arrows need to know exactly where the display is to be held and where the crowd will be. They want to know about any sensitive areas around the site, like hospitals, old people's homes, zoos and any other places which would be unduly disturbed by the aircraft. They must know of any hazards in the area, like cranes, towers or high tension cables and anything else that might affect, or be affected by, the display.

One very important thing to decide is the exact time for the Red Arrows' arrival. The Team may be appearing at three shows on the same day and they need to work out exactly when they can display at each place. This will, of course, have to tie in with other display teams which often have similar criteria, so there may be some negotiating to be done. When the questionnaire is completed it is returned to the Manager's office and goes into the relevant file. Each season, a separate file is opened for every display and, along with the questionnaire, this will eventually contain details of any correspondence, transport, accommodation and everything else concerned with that particular show.

If the Red Arrows are displaying at a site which they do not know or have not visited for the past three years, they must carry out a site survey. One of the pilots or the Team Manager will visit the site before the season starts, arrange to meet the organiser and discuss the display.

The pilot needs to see the display site, look at the terrain around it and check any hazards that must be avoided. Occasionally they might find they have been asked to display at a totally unsuitable site. An agricultural show might take place quite happily at the bottom of a valley, but the Red Arrows, unable to go down into it, would be virtually invisible to the crowds. It could suit a parachute display team perfectly, whereas the Red Arrows would be wasting both their time and the show's money.

The sites are classed A, B or C, according to their locations. Class A sites, where the Team have to fly over the paying public, need special dispensation for them to appear. Such displays have

largely been stopped although, in the past, the Team have displayed at Grand Prix venues, where they flew along the circuit and over some of the crowd. Biggin Hill, although surrounded by a built-up area, is only a category B site because although the Team fly over buildings, the only people who are under the display are those outside the airfield who have not paid for the privilege. A category C site is where the Team display over virtually uninhabited country or the sea.

Once all the details of the site have been checked, the information is put into the display file and, along with the completed questionnaire, is subsequently used by the Team Manager's staff to write the Operation Order. The "Op Order" is a standard format for each display, giving details of where the Team are going and how they are getting there, who is in charge (the Team Leader), who is going with them, who provides the aircraft, and all the take-off and landing times. It gives the meteorological requirements (when the Team need weather forecasts) and engineering requirements in terms of fuel, diesel and oxygen. Much of the information will simply be a formal confirmation of what has already been discussed. The Op Order is prepared about three weeks before a display and given to the Team Leader, the pilots, Engineering Officer, Support Command Headquarters, RAF Lyneham (when a Hercules transport aircraft is required to carry the ground crew and their equipment) and other people in the RAF who need to know exactly what the Team are doing. It also goes to the display organiser to confirm the timings and the Team's requirements, although he might not receive some of the more technical details included in the document.

In the week before the Red Arrows are due to appear the "WHAM" is prepared. This vital document was introduced to the Team by Squadron Leader Ploszek. It is distributed to all personnel who are going away and is an important part of the organisation. When Squadron Leader Ploszek first became Manager of the Red Arrows, he was constantly besieged by cries of "What's happening, Manager?" and so the WHAM was born. In greater

Right: An aerial map of the display site at Ramsey, Isle of Man, with datum, the display line, pull-up points and hazards marked. A Navigation Officer transfers this information from the Pitch map and gives them both to the Leader before the briefing. *British Crown Copyright/RAF Photograph*

Left: The 1986 Team listens to Squadron Leader
Richard Thomas as he briefs the 2,000th display at
Bournemouth's Hurn airport

Above: Flight Lieutenant Tony Lunnon-Wood climbs
into his cockpit before the display. The Synchro Pair
wear anti-*g* suits over their flying suits to prevent them
blacking out during their manoeuvres

detail than the Op Order, it concentrates on every-thing the pilots and ground crew need to know while they are on the road. The WHAM tells them all the timings they will need to be in the right place at the right time, and information about recep-tions, eating arrangements and hotels where they will be staying. It gives the names and telephone numbers of contacts who can help them and detailed briefing and take-off times. Everyone knows exactly what they should be doing – and no-one knows quite how they managed in the old days.

As the date of the display approaches, Synchro Lead (the pilot leading the Synchronised Pair, the two aircraft which perform the series of breath-taking crosses during the second half of the show) will take out the appropriate file and draw up a map of the display site. The maps of Britain and Western Europe are all stored in the "Nav/Planning" room at Scampton, although the Flight Planning Clerk will have to resort to a central map store, a map research establishment, or even an embassy if the Team are displaying at an unusual foreign site. Synchro Lead will take out a 50,000:1 scale map of the display area and transfer all the information about the site from the display file onto it. He then decides on the display line, datum (the central point along the crowd line, at which the whole display is orientated) and any reference headings which he and Synchro 2 will be using. Three copies of this "Pitch map" are made, two for the Synchro pilots and one for the Team Leader. The Team Leader's copy goes first to the two pilots who are also the Navigation Officers for that season. These pilots, known as Nav 1 and 2, must then work out the routes and timings to ensure that the Team arrive over the crowds at exactly the right moment.

The Red Arrows always arrive from behind the crowd at 90° to the display line so the Navs work backwards, plotting out the route from the display site back to the airfield from which the Team will be taking off. Even if the Team are displaying over an airfield on which they are based, they will ini-tially have to take off, fly away from the site and then position and turn to give themselves a proper

approach. The Team Leader wants to have about a seven mile straight run-in for the display and, no matter how far they have come, expects to arrive on time. "We aim to arrive plus or minus five seconds," said Squadron Leader Pete Collins, who joined for the 1986 season and was made Nav 2 the following year. "The boss was really upset if we were eight or ten seconds early, but in fact you could normally set your watch by us."

The Navs mark the run-in line at ten second intervals, so that the Team Leader, using his stop-watch, will know exactly where he is supposed to be at each interval. He can then vary his speed according to the wind, to ensure a punctual arrival.

At the beginning of this line, an Initial Point (IP) is marked with a precise time, using a road, river or other landmark, and this is where the Leader will turn for the run-in. At this point he will also swap from a 500,000:1 scale map to the 50,000:1. The Navs will have used the smaller scale map to plot the route across the country back to the roll point on the airfield.

Depending on the display time, the Navs will work out an exact roll time for the Team. The aircraft may take off at 13.28 and 17 seconds for a two o'clock display – it is that precise. The Navs know that when they roll, the Team will need two minutes to take off and accelerate to transitting speed and then be four miles from base. The Team usually transit within Britain at 360 knots (six miles a minute), so they mark the route between the four mile point and the IP at six mile intervals.

Unfortunately they cannot simply fly from airfield to display site in a straight line. The air space above much of Britain and Europe is rigidly controlled and the Navs have to work around any restricted areas when they are planning the route. These areas can be anything from bird sanctuaries, large towns, hang glider sites, or castles owned by the Queen, to civilian and military air traffic zones, gunnery sites or firing ranges. In general the Team prefer to keep away from controlled areas – because there is always the danger that they might be held up and prevented from making the display time – but that is not always possible.

The Team Leader may not see the maps until five minutes before Briefing – about half an hour before take-off. He will be briefed by the Navs about the route and the weather and by Synchro Lead about any hazards or obstacles at the display site. This information will then be passed on to the rest of the Team during their Briefing from the Leader just before departure.

During the flight, the Team Leader takes over the actual navigation, using the maps and varying the speed if necessary to ensure the formation gets to the right places at the right times.

On a normal low level transit within Britain, he will use only UHF frequency on his radio, which keeps him in radio contact with the rest of the Team, while leaving the Navigation Officers to listen on UHF but also use VHF to talk to the "ground". The Navs will each be talking to the controllers of any air traffic zones which the Team are flying through or near. Even if they are simply flying around a controlled zone they will still make a courtesy call to let the ground know that the Red Arrows formation is passing – so that the Team can be told of any unexpected activity on their route. Sometimes the Navs will have contacted the controllers in advance, but this is usually only necessary if the Team need to do something out of the ordinary. They will normally call up on the radio during the flight and Nav 1 may talk to the controllers of one zone, while Nav 2 is talking to another.

If the display is to take place during an air show, as the formation approaches the display site one of the Navs must get clearance to display. He will also get details of the local weather and wind speeds and relay the information to the Leader. Throughout the display, while the rest of the Team are tuned in to the leader on UHF, the Operating Nav must also listen on VHF in case the local controllers suddenly need to speak to him. They will usually keep quiet during the display unless something unexpected happens, but, as one Navigation Officer said ruefully, "It doesn't always work like that."

Wherever the Team display, a NOTAM – a Notice to Airmen – goes to all civil and military air traffic zones, asking them to keep clear of the area up to about 6,000 feet for the period of the display, plus ten minutes at each end.

The Team Manager, commentating on the ground, is also in radio contact with the Team on UHF. This means that if the display site is not at an airfield, the Manager can give the Team information about the wind and anything else they might need. It also enables him to know exactly when the Team will arrive and what they are doing – especially necessary during unsettled weather, when the Leader is forced to change the display.

The Team can only fly their full spectacular display, incorporating loops and rolls, if the cloud base is no lower than 4,500 feet and visibility is good. If the cloud base is between 2,500 and 4,500 feet, they give a rolling display which includes rolls but not the high loops. If the English weather is even worse with a cloud base between 1,000 and 2,500 feet, the Team will perform a series of passes in front of the crowd in different formations in what is known as their flat show. If the weather is changeable, the Team Leader may be going from full to flat and back again several times during one display.

*   *   *

The Red Arrows always spend some time each season at air shows abroad. When they are transiting from Britain to the continent the Team fly at high level along the same routes as the commercial airliners. The Navigation Officers will still talk to the ground, but the Leader will also listen in as the timings are not so critical.

The criteria for accepting invitations to display abroad tend to be different from those in Britain. There is little chance of attracting RAF recruits at small aero-clubs in West Germany, although the public relations exercise may be very important. The club's members and civilians living nearby might well have had to put up with a great deal of low flying from RAF Harriers stationed in the region. A Red Arrows display is a way of thanking

Overleaf: An Apollo Loop over the Gloucestershire countryside

them and maybe reducing the number of complaints the following year.

The Team are also often invited to appear at big air shows on the Continent. One regular venue is the United States Air Force Base at Ramstein in West Germany. In 1986 their *Flugtag* (Air Day) offered both the Service families and the German public the opportunity to look round hundreds of different aircraft and see many of them perform. The spectators were thrilled by the F16s and astonished by the versatility of the Harrier; but the Red Arrows were, for many, the highlight of the day. Their appearance helped attract over 300,000 people to the air show – a contrast to the previous day when the Team had displayed in Italy, to a much smaller, though very appreciative, crowd of scantily clad Italian holidaymakers. The organisers of that show in Rimini had benefited from a problem in the previous season.

The Red Arrows had been invited to appear at Rivolto in Italy to celebrate the twenty-fifth anniversary of the Italian aerobatic team, the *Frecce Tricolori*. Although the Red Arrows were on the continent that weekend and based only thirty minutes flying time away, they were already committed to a display in West Germany and could not do both. They have a very good relationship with the Italian team and it caused some embarrassment, so it was decided that the Team must make a diplomatic appearance in Italy the following year and Rimini was lucky.

One very important reason for displaying abroad is to boost defence sales and for this reason the Red Arrows sometimes go even further afield than Europe. A country which is trying to decide which aircraft to buy for advanced jet training might well be swayed by the British Aerospace Hawk, when it sees nine of them performing with consummate precision in its skies.

In 1981 the Red Arrows toured the Middle East for thirty-one days in the spring, before returning to England to start the season there. The trip was a great success and they performed in many different countries including a display in Jordan in front of King Hussein. He presented them with the Royal

Order of the Hashemite Kingdom: a beautiful wide gold chain encrusted with jewels, which can be seen alongside other gifts, in a glass case in the Red Arrows reception area at RAF Scampton.

The trip began after the Red Arrows had spent their usual two weeks in Cyprus completing their winter training. However, shortly after the Team had arrived there, the Leader, Brian Hoskins, thought that their final practices might not proceed quite as smoothly as he had hoped. The Team were staying in the Officers' Mess and, as was often the case, they began to spend time in the snooker room each evening, playing "Tanks" around the table. Tanks is an old favourite, played throughout the Services, and needs a snooker table, two teams, two snooker balls and a great deal of running about. It can get very rough and noisy and in Cyprus, where the snooker table was in a small room and had a tiled floor which became slippery if drinks were spilled, it also got quite dangerous. After a couple of days and a couple of the Team members being knocked over in the scramble, Brian Hoskins decided he had better warn the pilots to be careful. He did so, saying that he was afraid that one of them would fall, really hurt themselves and jeopardise the coming tour.

That same afternoon, Brian Hoskins went to be interviewed on the local Forces radio. When he returned and went into the dining room for dinner, he was met by three of the other pilots. One of them, Neil Wharton, had his arm in plaster. "It went right from his wrist to his biceps," said Brian Hoskins. "He was looking very sheepish and said that they had played Tanks that afternoon, and exactly what I had warned them against had happened. Someone had spilled their beer, he had slipped on the wet floor and broken his arm.

"I wasn't absolutely convinced. I sat down to dinner and thought about it. It was the sort of prank that Wharty would get up to, but I wasn't sure. It looked right and was obviously a genuine plaster cast. He seemed very upset and one of the other guys was cutting up the meat for him.

"After I had finished I got up to leave and they asked where I was going. I said that I was going to telephone back to UK to see if the chap who'd flown in Neil Wharton's position the previous year could come out and join the Team. We had to be able to display in public in two weeks' time and that was, in fact, what I would probably have had to do if he really had broken his arm – and if he hadn't, it would call his bluff. I then went, got a cup of coffee and sat down to read a newspaper but I was beginning to think I would have to make that call.

"Apparently they went into panic stations. They raced down to the medical centre where they had persuaded the doctor to put the perfectly good arm in plaster. He wasn't there. The guys had thought that they would keep it up until about ten o'clock, when the doctor said he would cut the plaster off – it was only eight and the medical orderly who was there refused to remove it. The pilots ended up in the Officers' Mess kitchen, hacking at it with a bread knife. Because it had been done so professionally, it was very difficult to get off. They eventually succeeded – after cutting his arm in the process – and then came to tell me it was all a joke. But it was very, very well done and I had been worried."

In 1983 the Red Arrows were invited to go to the United States of America to help celebrate the bi-centenary of manned flight at Andrews Air Force Base, Washington. They went via Scotland, Greenland and Canada, took three and a half weeks and covered 11,500 miles.

At the time the Red Arrows went to the United States, the US Navy wanted to buy four hundred aircraft and was deciding between the Hawk and some other similar jets. Shortly after the Red Arrows' tour, they bought the Hawk. It may have been a coincidence, but the Team's visit had been very well received.

In 1986 the Red Arrows undertook their most ambitious trip yet. They had been asked if it was possible to take the Team out to Indonesia to display at an air show in Jakarta, which would mark the tenth anniversary of the Indonesian aircraft industry.

The Indonesians had decided to hold an air show every ten years, and as this was to be the first

it seemed a good idea to invite the Red Arrows to participate. The initial approach was made between government officials who saw no problems – the organisation only took ten months to complete.

The first step was to devise a route which would take the aircraft out to Indonesia as quickly as possible. The Hawk is a very economical aircraft and flying at 37,000 feet, the Team aimed to cover an average of 800 miles on each transit. They decided to avoid displaying on the way to Jakarta in order to ensure that they arrived with at least nine serviceable aircraft for the main aim of the trip, the Far East Air Show. On the way back they planned to offer displays to the countries through which they had passed.

Although the Team would be transitting through many different countries, the routes were planned in a similar way to flights within Britain and Europe. The main differences were that the navigation planning began two and a half *months* before the Team left, rather than the usual two weeks, and that every flight plan had to have a diplomatic clearance number on it to say that each embassy had cleared the Team to go into their air space. In addition, the Flight Planning Clerk, in his first season with the Team, spent many hours tracking down maps for the Team to use, and if the usual sources failed, he had to resort to asking the relevant embassies. Despite his work and the preparation done by the Navs, the Synchro Pair still had to draw their own map on a scrap of paper, complete with headings and reference points, to fly one display.

All the general organisation was done through the air attachés in the countries concerned. They approached each government and asked if they would like the Red Arrows to display. When the Team had established where the shows would be, they sent out representatives, usually the Team Manager and the Engineering Officer, to do the equivalent of the site survey. They told the relevant air attachés that they were coming and the attachés arranged for them to meet the organisers of the air shows. They held meetings to discuss the Red Arrows' requirements and looked at the display site in just the same way as they would have done for a new venue in Britain.

Accommodation was usually arranged through the air attachés, although during the recces Squadron Leader Ploszek realised that good discounts and extras could be negotiated with many Far Eastern hotels and he became adept at haggling. In addition to the usual embassy discounts he managed to get even better terms from some hotels for the "world famous aerobatic team" and promises of flowers, fruit and drinks in their rooms on arrival. In the end the pilots voted the Bangkok Hilton the best hotel on the trip – but this may have been in contrast to their earlier experiences in Jakarta where the pilots found themselves crossing open sewers to get to their hotel.

It was not until the week before departure that

Above: Flight Lieutenant Charlie McIlroy, a Synchro pilot in 1986 and 1987, waiting to taxi

Right: The Team Manager, Squadron Leader Henry Ploszek, waits in the commentator's box for the Team to arrive and begin the display

the Team had the final approval for the trip. This meant that in addition to the months and months of preparation for the six-week tour, they also had to plan a contingency schedule of displays in Britain in case the Indonesian visit failed to go ahead.

When the Red Arrows finally arrived in Jakarta, they were told that the French organisers were insisting that the teams keep to French rules for aerobatic displays. These included the stipulation about not flying over the crowd at any stage during the show. For a time it looked as though the Arrows had gone all that way and would return without displaying, until eventually government officials became involved and the organisers were overruled.

The Red Arrows performed their display as usual and held the Indonesians spellbound. Almost one million people turned up to see an aerobatic team which many of them had never heard of and very few had seen. The months of preparation paid off and the Team had very few problems. The aircraft performed very well, even in the extremes of temperature to which they were exposed, and the only casualty was one of the ground crew who had to be flown back suffering from sunstroke.

Although it was hardly reported in Britain, the whole trip was a great success. The Royal Air Force Aerobatic Team, the Red Arrows, had flown further than ever before and were seen by many people who knew little about Britain or the RAF. The long transit out to the Far East was kept quiet to ensure there were no problems with terrorists but as they returned, displaying in countries as diverse as Thailand and Pakistan, the pilots were sorry that such a successful tour still received little publicity in Britain – one of the national papers told the RAF that unfortunately the Team were too good to be news. They did not make enough mistakes.

★   ★   ★

During every show at which the Red Arrows appear, whether in Britain or abroad, the Team Manager must be on the ground at the display site to give the commentary to the crowd and keep in touch with the Team by radio. Getting to the commentary position is no problem at air shows held on large airfields where the Red Arrows are based for the weekend. The Team fly in initially with ten aircraft, the Spare flown by the Team Manager. They all land and when their display time approaches the pilots take off and the manager goes to the commentary position. Things are, however, a little more complicated when the display is to be over a small, perhaps grass only, airfield. The Hawk aircraft cannot land and so they are based somewhere nearby.

The Team Manager will land his aircraft with the other jets, jump into a Bulldog, a two-seater trainer, with the Team photographer and his video, take off for the display site and land to wait for the Team to appear. The Hawks, meanwhile, are refuelled and prepared for the display. The pilots take off, do the show (while the Manager commentates on the ground) and they then return to their base. As soon as the display is finished, the Manager will get back into the Bulldog and return to rejoin the Team and pick up his jet.

The Bulldogs belong to University Air Squadrons (UAS) around the country. When the Manager is working out the display timetables, he looks to see when he will need to borrow one and then tells the UAS Headquarters. They go to the local areas and "task" the Universities to move their aeroplane into position for him. ("I think in civilian life you would probably say 'ask'!") A few days before the display the squadron rings the Manager to confirm the arrangement.

During the season the Red Arrows often display at sites over the sea or over other places where there is no airfield at all. In this case, Support Command Headquarters are asked to provide a Gazelle helicopter and they task the helicopter side of the Central Flying School, based at Shawbury. The Manager is picked up from where the jets are based and flown to the display site. He will have contacted the organisers of the show and asked them to provide a landing site for the helicopter, perhaps a football ground or playing fields. He will also need a police escort and a car to take him through the traffic to the display site. Time is always critical as he must be in radio contact with the Team and be in position to introduce them as they arrive over the crowd. After the commentary, the Manager is taken back through the traffic to the helicopter and he then rejoins the Team.

"Shawbury also have a helicopter display pilot who sometimes goes to the same shows," says Squadron Leader Ploszek. "Last season I had arranged for a Bulldog to be left for me at USAF Mildenhall where we were based for the weekend. The team were displaying at Southend on the Monday and I realised that the display helicopter would be passing right by on his way to the show. Rather than waste fuel, I arranged for him to collect me on the way, drop me at Southend while he did his display and I commentated for the Team. He then picked me up again and left me at Mildenhall on his way back to Shawbury."

Whenever the Team stay away from home, the accommodation is the responsibility of the Team Manager. In the early years he and his staff used to contact each hotel personally and arrange the bookings, but since 1984 they have used the services of Expotel, a professional firm. They know how much the Team can spend on accommodation and they contact the hotels and negotiate prices for the block bookings. They have to arrange not only for the pilots and the Manager to stay, but also for the large number of engineers needed to keep the aeroplanes flying. If they are accompanied by a Hercules, which is used to carry ground crew and equipment, they will need seventeen singles for the officers (which includes the Engineering Officer and the six Hercules crew) and fifteen twin rooms for the ground crew. The officers and the airmen usually stay in separate hotels – not usually different standards, just different – which enables everyone to relax and enjoy themselves off-duty.

Every practice and every display is video-taped by the Team's photographer. He is part of first-line engineering, the men who service the aircraft when the Team are away, although his trade is that of photographer rather than engineer. He travels with the ground crew in the Hercules and accompanies the Manager when he does the commentaries. He does not usually fly in the back of the Manager's Hawk, but will go with him in a Bulldog or Gazelle helicopter, if that is how the Manager is travelling to the commentary position.

Before each display the Team meet and the Team Leader briefs the pilots, telling them the wind speeds, weather, any hazards to avoid, nearby airfields to use in emergency and any details of the display to note. At Scampton they will brief in the Briefing Room next to their Crew Room. When they are away they will usually meet at "five's" – around the wing of Red 5's aeroplane. If it is pouring with rain, it makes a convenient if uncomfortable shelter.

When each practice or display is over the Team will de-brief, running through everything that has happened. If they are at home or they can get facilities, they play the video through immediately so they can see how they have performed. If one of the aircraft is not quite in perfect formation, the pilot may have to put up with some banter but there is usually not much said – they can all see what is wrong and the pilot concerned knows exactly what he should do. If there are several displays on one day and no facilities for playing the video, the team may have to wait until they arrive at their hotel, but they always run through each display carefully. It is this constant attention to detail which keeps the display tight and perfectly controlled.

It is only after all the background organisation has been done, the sites surveyed, the routes planned and the hotels booked that the Red Arrows can appear in front of the public. The planning has to be meticulous; when you are dealing with millions of pounds worth of aircraft and nine highly trained pilots, you cannot afford to make mistakes. It is a point of pride with the Team that they always arrive over the crowd at exactly the right time, immediately after the Team Manager has said, "Ladies and Gentlemen, I present the Red Arrows."

CHAPTER THREE
REDS, ROLLING, NOW!

This section shows a typical display from the pilots' point of view. In their own words, and using the diagrams to follow the manoeuvres, it chronicles the thoughts, radio calls and actions of the Team Leader and Synchro Lead that produce the display itself.

TEAM LEADER
"We want to achieve an exact roll time. From the taxi out I'm looking at my watch the whole time. We must arrive on the runway with about a minute and a half to sit there before we release the brakes. The time we check in on the radio and the taxying speed are both critical.
Out on the runway, everybody is getting into position behind me. I'm looking at the time and watching the seconds tick away. I hear

'ALL ABOARD!' from No. 9 and know that they're all lined up. Thirty seconds to go to roll time, I call,
'SMOKE!' which reminds them to check that their smoke master switches are on.
'LIGHTS ON, GO!'
'POWER!'
Pushing the throttle up to take-off power, I'm checking left and right to make sure Nos 2 and 3 are ready. I assume they are all ready down the back – they'll tell me if they're not.
Three seconds to go, press transmit button.
Two seconds, I call,
'REDS!'
One second,
'ROLLING!', and as the hand sweeps through the right time,
'NOW!' "

Above: Squadron Leader Ploszek gives a brief history of the Team before they arrive for their annual display at RAF Biggin Hill

Right: Lined up and ready to taxi

Formations during the Display

1 Big Nine
"Ladies and Gentlemen, I present the Red Arrows", and the Team arrive from behind the crowd trailing white smoke in Big Nine formation to begin the display

2 Diamond Nine
has become the Red Arrows' trademark and this formation appears, with their motto *éclat* (brilliant), on their squadron badge. All their other formations are developed from this basic pattern

5 Viggen
This formation is named after the famous air-defence fighter. Nos 2 and 3 represent the small canard winglets which were fitted to it

6
Nos 8 and 9 move back to form the shape of the **Feathered Arrow** – too much of a mouthful to be used over the radio, this is always shortened to Fred

7 Apollo
After Viggen the rear four aircraft move forward to form Apollo, named after the early space capsule

11 Big Seven
As the Synchro Pair begin their manoeuvres the remaining seven aircraft form into Big Seven and dive through the heart-shape formed by the Synchro's smoke, fanning out in a Cascade

12 Swan
After the Synchro Pair have completed their Opposition Barrel Rolls, the seven aircraft roll in front of the crowd in Swan formation

3 Wineglass
is a difficult formation for the pilots on the outside, Nos 4 and 5. As the Team roll they have to work very hard to maintain the straight line

4 Nine Arrow
Nos 8 and 9 move out to complete the Arrow for Nine Arrow

10 Leader's Benefit
Another difficult formation to fly as the Team have to maintain the straight line. This is the point at which the Synchro Pair split from the rest of the Team to form the heart and begin the second half of the show

8 Card Nine
A very difficult formation to fly for the pilots on the outside and at the back as they work to keep the lines straight

9 Concorde
Flown in celebration of the supersonic airliner, with Nos 8 and 9 at the back representing the engines

13/14 Seven Arrow and Box
are basically the same formation with Nos 2, 3, 4 and 5 flying in different positions

15 Vixen
is named after the famous Royal Navy fighter aircraft – and the Vixen Break, where the aircraft split suddenly in front of the crowd, is the most severe of the main formation's manoeuvres

"Down the runway, watch the acceleration, check the instruments. At 95 knots, nose wheel off. Not very high nose attitude, speed increases 110, 120, hold the aircraft on the runway, then at 130 knots, little check back on the stick and we're off the ground. Landing gear and flaps up immediately we're airborne.

Speed increasing to 155 knots and I throttle back. Nos 4 and 5 can then join on the outside of the formation, and the back four who have taken off a little behind us can catch up. So I throttle back to about 92%, depending on temperature. Holding it fairly level, fairly low, speed gradually increases to 200 knots. At about 200 knots, Red 6, leading the rear section, calls,

'AIR BRAKES GO!'

Nos 4 and 5 put their smoke on and No. 6 calls

'TURN!'

Power comes back up to 96%, then pull up, wing over to the left today.

Turning left, back section joins up and I hear

'ALL ABOARD!' from No. 6.

All smoke off and formation is complete.

Down behind the crowd, increase speed to 340 knots then call,

'THROTTLING BACK!'

I set the power now, 92% as it's a fairly cool English summer's day. That should see me through the display. If I set it accurately the speed should virtually take care of itself. I don't want to keep moving the throttle because that makes it difficult for the people at the back to hang on to. As we come round from crowd rear for the start of the display, I call,

'SMOKE ON, GO!'"

Right: Reds, Rolling, Now!

Arrival . . . and Big Nine Loop . . .

"Arriving from crowd rear in Big 9 formation. Before I pull up on any loop, I check to make sure we have looping speed. In Britain in our temperatures anything from 330 to 370 is acceptable. We don't want the loops too big, so I try to keep the speed down; 340, 350 knots. That's fine. Power is set, now the most important thing is the g [the apparent increase in the force of gravity caused by the aircraft changing direction] on entry into the loop. Start pulling nice and smoothly, 2, 3, 3½. Hold 3½g.

'DIAMOND, GO!'

And the acknowledgements, '6! 7!'

Six people have to move during that change, but Nos 6 and 7 are the prime movers and they come right in behind me. Nobody moves until they have acknowledged my calls so we all know that they have heard me.

Hold 3½g, I'm looking at the artificial horizon, pulling up to the vertical, then backing the g off very slightly. Getting to the vertical, check speed, 230, 220 knots. I don't want it to go below 200 or it will be very slow over the top.

215 knots in the vertical, look left out of the window to get the pitch. If you linger, you run out of speed very quickly. I'm looking backwards and as the horizon starts to come back in over the top of my head, I reduce the pull but ensure that the nose does continue to pitch down.

Over the top there is less than 1g so it's a little bit of a float. It gives everybody at the back a bit in hand. So going over the top, I look at the height. This is critical, if I'm too low I'll end up having problems on the pull out. But if we start with the correct entry g and the correct speed, we'll go over the top at about the right height, between 4,600 and 5,300 feet. The bumpier it is, the bigger the loop because it is difficult to get a steady g on entry. I like to get it round about 4,700 because that's quite nice and tight.

Over the top of the arrival loop,

'COMING RIGHT, NOW!'

Starting to apply bank to the right because we're coming into the Diamond bend.

'SMOKE OFF, GO!'

Pointing directly at datum so the crowd can't actually see the cut off. Coming to 45° line away from datum and as soon as I'm there,

'REVERSING LEFT, NOW!'

Coming left and in for a flat 360° turn, looking at speed, looking at height. Height decreases as we come towards datum to make it look as though we're doing a flat turn. In fact it's a descending turn all the way to datum. As the nose goes through datum, for the Diamond bend, I call,

'SMOKE ON, GO!'

I don't usually call for any particular colour smoke, I just say 'SMOKE ON, GO!' They know which colour they should use.

Getting to the 45° line, away from the crowd,

'AND REVERSING!' (from the left hand turn to a right hand turn).

Slow reversal, and as we reverse,

'SMOKE OFF, GO!'

Up into wing over, as soon as the bank is set, nose in the right position, it is time for the change to Feathered Arrow ('Fred').

'FRED, GO!'

And the acknowledgement,

'8! 9!'

Smoke comes on automatically on the change, then 'SMOKE OFF, GO!' from No. 9 because he is coming back into position and can see when the change is complete."

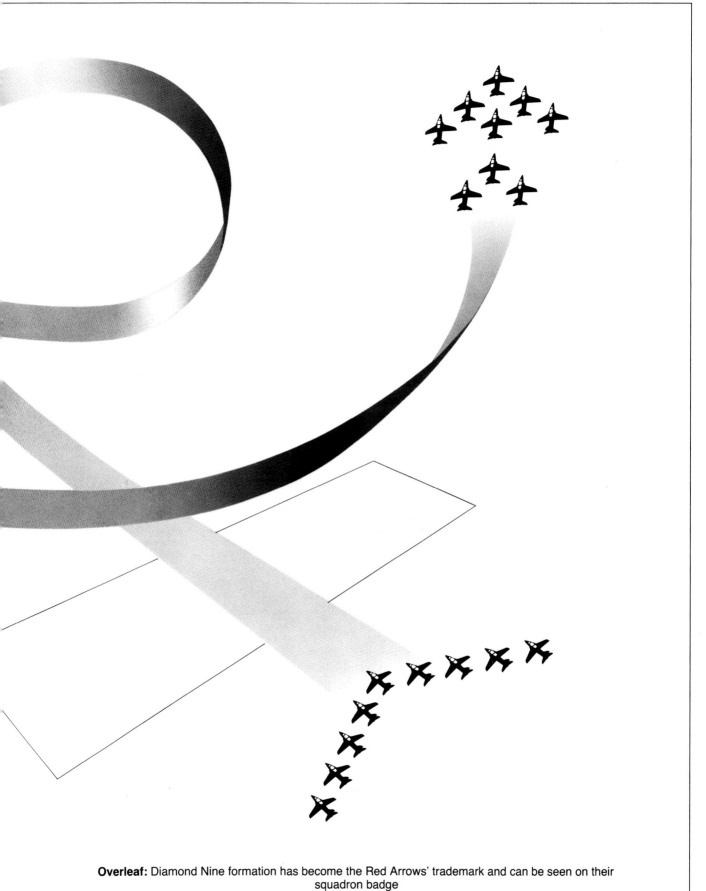

Overleaf: Diamond Nine formation has become the Red Arrows' trademark and can be seen on their squadron badge

Wineglass Roll . . .

"Coming down, pointing towards the crowd, coming in for the Wineglass Roll,
'BANK COMING OFF A BIT!'
This gives a better entry for Nos 4 and 5 who have been working hardest on the outside.
'WINEGLASS, GO!'
'2! 3!'
Wineglass is difficult because the front five are in a straight line, you have no reference to tell you exactly how far away you are from the aircraft next to you. You don't look at wing tips, so Nos 2 and 3 have to get the line abreast sorted out exactly for everyone else to line up heads and make sure we do get a straight line.
'SMOKE ON, GO!'
'PULLING UP!'

As I start to pull up, I begin to feed the bank on very slowly to the left, looking for wings level at 25° of pitch, which I take from the attitude indicator. When I get there,
'AND ROLLING!'
I don't want to roll too quickly because that gives big problems to Nos 4 and 5 who are on the outside. They haven't got much power in hand, if I don't get it just right they'll drop back. At the top of the roll, I'm looking at the speed, about 230 knots, and looking at the height which should be about 2,500 feet. I'm assessing the rate of roll, trying to keep it the same all the way round. Then,
'HOLDING BANK, NOW!' to set up the next manoeuvre.
'FRED, GO!'
'2! 3!'"

Overleaf: A Wineglass caught in evening sunlight

Nine Arrow . . .

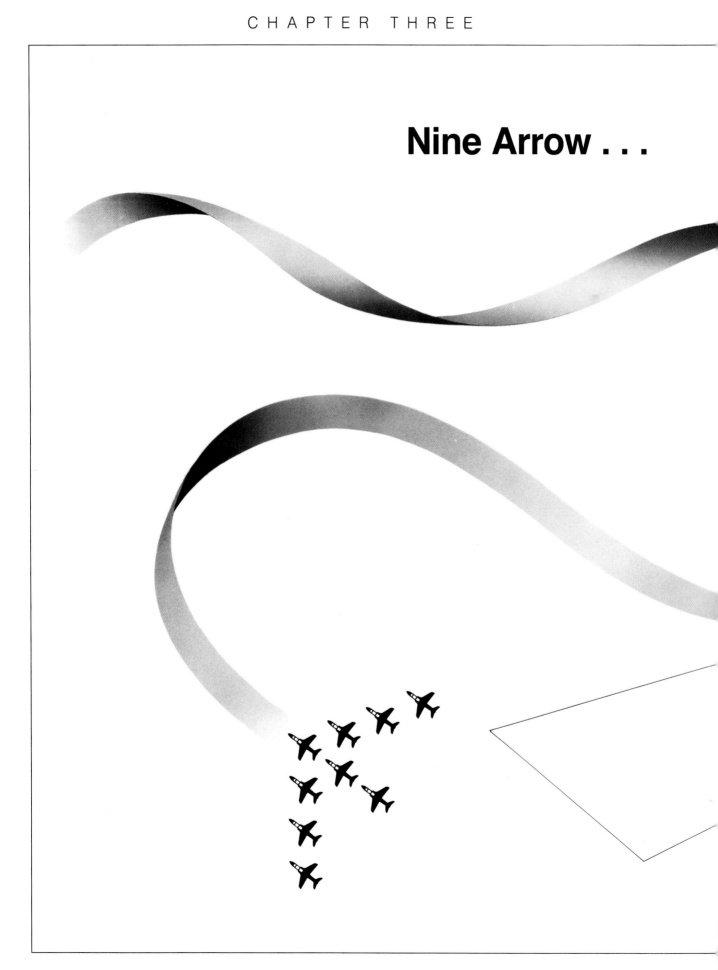

to Diamond Loop . . .

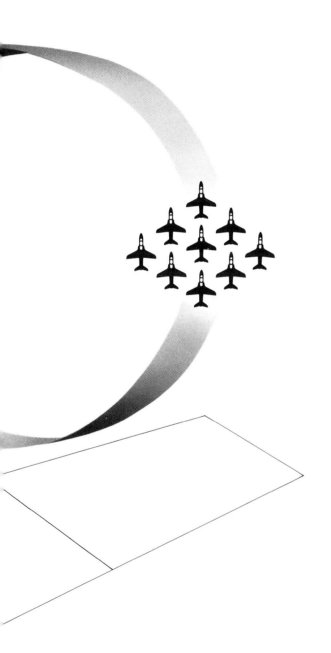

"Then,
'SMOKE OFF, GO!'
'MORE BANK!'
'TIGHTENING!'
(Which increases the rate of turn and this increases the *g*.)
'NINE ARROW, GO!'
'8! 9!'
Throughout all this the speed is fairly steady. For the rolls you are looking for 330 knots, and that is checked before the roll begins. There's no point in pulling up and thinking 'Oh no, I haven't got the speed.' I monitor it the whole time so I know well in advance if I could be hard up for speed.
Changing to Nine Arrow, coming to 90° looking at the crowd,
'ROLLING OUT!'
Checking speed, checking power, steady pull to 3½*g*. As soon as *g* is established,
'DIAMOND, GO!'
'8! 9!'
Up over the top,
'WHITE ON, GO!'
Everybody changes from colour to white at the back. When I'm upside down I call,
'COMING RIGHT, NOW!'
Rolling the bank on very slowly as I bend the loop and end up going away from datum on the 45° line.
'AND REVERSING!'
'SMOKE OFF, GO!'"

Overleaf: The red and white markings on the underbellies of the Hawks can clearly be seen as they perform a Diamond Loop

Viggen Roll . . .

"The reversal takes us back to a left hand turn. As
the bank is set in a left turn,
'VIGGEN, GO!'
'4! 5!'
They drop back, Nos 8 and 9 stay in position until
No. 5 says,
'GO!'
Then Nos 8 and 9 drop back. This gives a tidy, neat
change. The whole change is complete and No. 5
who has the whole formation in his sight says,
'SMOKE OFF, GO!'
'BANK COMING OFF A BIT!'
I settle myself for the roll,
'SMOKE ON, GO!'
'PULLING UP!'
Once again, 25° of pitch, wings level and the roll
begins.
Round we go, down the other side and as we get to
the far end so everybody will know there's *g*
coming on.
'PULLING UP!'
'SMOKE OFF, GO!' "

Overleaf: 330 knots down the runway to begin a Viggen Roll

Card Loop . . .

" 'COMING LEFT, NOW!'
Change to left hand turn and then,
'APOLLO, GO!'
'8! 9!'
No. 5 says,
'SMOKE OFF, GO!'
Coming round the corner for the change to Card,
'CARD, GO!'
'4! 5!'
This is a difficult manoeuvre for Nos 4, 5 and 7 who
are at the back. It's not so bad for the front six but at
the back it is very difficult to get the lines right. I
must make absolutely sure that we are pointing
directly at datum otherwise it doesn't look right.
'SMOKE ON, GO!'
Pause.
'PULLING UP!'
Check speed, check power, $3\frac{1}{2}g$. All the way up,
then in the vertical,
'APOLLO, GO!'
'4! 5!'
They move to the outside at the top,
'SMOKE OFF, GO!'
Coming over the top, apply a little bit of bank to
the left to allow us to come in for the Apollo Bend.
'SMOKE ON, GO!' and then,
'COMING RIGHT, NOW!'
Start to apply bank to the right as we descend to
pass datum at 250 feet. It can be difficult to get to
the right place at the right height without giving
them a difficult ride."

Overleaf left: The Hawks climb up into a Card Loop, generally agreed by the pilots to be one of the most difficult formations to fly perfectly

Overleaf right: Apollo formation was named after the early space capsule

. . . into the Concorde bend . . .

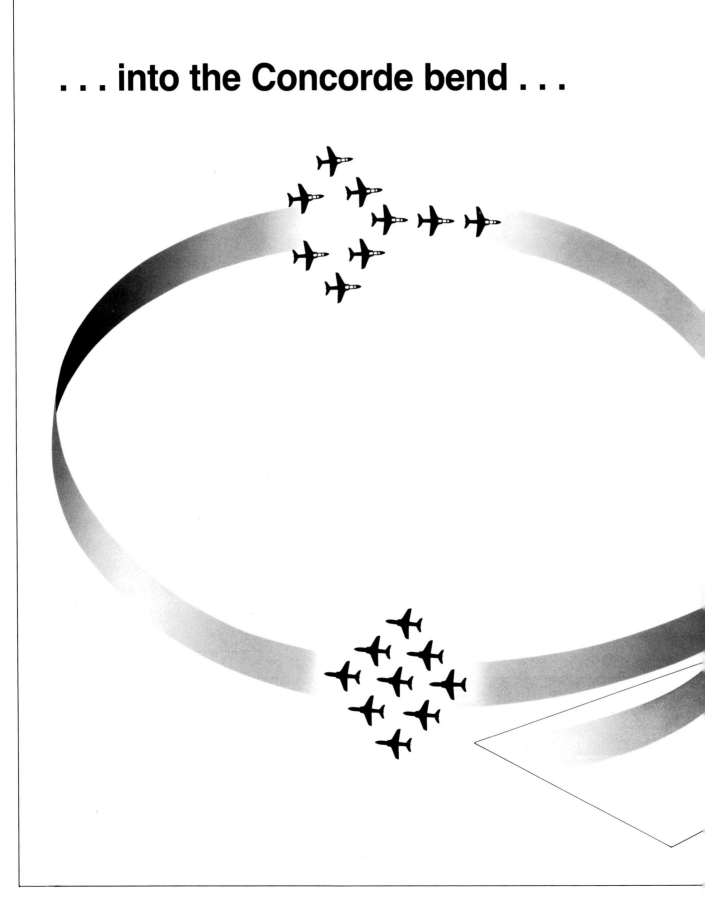

"As soon as we're past datum,
'DIAMOND, GO!'
Nos 4 and 5 move forwards. We're doing that with tail pipes on to the crowd so that they don't see the change. The smoke goes off automatically on that call.
Round the corner,
'CONCORDE, GO!'
'2! 3!'
Increase power by 2%. The rest drop back and I glance in the mirrors to see how they are doing. I don't need to, it's just out of interest, idle curiosity.

I can't tell exact positions but it gives me an idea of how it's going. Once the change is complete, from No. 5,
'SMOKE OFF, GO!'
More bank as we come round the corner, pointing towards datum,
'SMOKE ON, GO!'
'TIGHTENING!' just to give it a nice crack as we go past datum.
As soon as we're past,
'LETTING IT OUT!' (which reduces the g).
'ROLLING OUT!'"

Overleaf: Smoke from the Concorde's engines billows out across the sky

. . . to Feathered Arrow Loop . . .

"As soon as the wings are level,
'PULLING UP!'
'FRED, GO!'
'2! 3!'
Because I want to get the next change over as soon as possible. Holding quite a lot of power up over the loop, I can see people coming forward and Nos 2 and 3 are back alongside me, just about to go upside down,
'THROTTLING BACK!'
To a normal looping power and this gives the people at the back a bit in hand.
'LETTING IT OUT!' and then,
'SMOKE OFF, GO!'
'COMING RIGHT, NOW!'
Turning right.
'TIGHTENING!'
'NINE ARROW, GO!'
'8! 9!' "

Overleaf: Feathered Arrow is the official name of the formation; the pilots shorten it to Fred

Leader's Benefit, Split and Cascade . . .

" 'LEADER'S BENEFIT, GO!' – and everybody puts their smoke on.
'ROLLING OUT!'
Leader's Benefit is tricky just at the beginning of the loop so you have got to be very steady on the pull because depth is critical. If people go deep in their slot or shallow, it shows up and the line gets distorted. As soon as the wings become level,
'SPLIT, GO!'
Synchro Pair split from the rest of the formation. There is no acknowledgement but here I must look in the mirrors to make sure Nos 6 and 7 have cleared. Watch them go, both of them, through the mirrors, check speed, 350 knots, check power, 92%.
'PULLING UP!'
$3\frac{1}{2}g$."

SYNCHRO
"I'm pulling up away from the main formation, a nice steady pull so Synchro 2 can hang on. I want at least 2,300 feet before I start the heart so we can get a nice peaky bottom to it. At 2,300 feet, I call,
'SPLIT, GO!'
On goes the smoke. Roll away from Synchro 2; 3,700, 4,000, 4,300 feet and over the top, looking across to try and match the sides of the heart."

LEADER
"Coming to the vertical,
'BIG SEVEN, GO!'
'4! 5!'
As we get to the top of the loop, I'm looking at the Synchro Pair and watching the start of the heart. In the vertical on the way down, I'm looking as far ahead as I can. I need to get exactly on a line for datum so that when I call the Fan, I've got the line absolutely right. If I alter it at all after I've called it, we'll end up with a Fan (or Cascade) which is not evenly spaced."

SYNCHRO
"We're coming down towards the ground, exactly parallel to the crowd. Looking at Synchro 2, coming closer, smoke off automatically and we're past with a right to right cross to complete the heart. As I'm approaching the bottom, I'm looking for threshold [points 3,000 feet either side of datum]. When the boss has called the Fan, I'll know if the timing is right."

LEADER
"'FAN, FAN . . . GO!'
No acknowledgement, down we go. I can hear
Synchro making their calls.
At the bottom,
'SMOKE OFF, GO!'
And we start the pull up to make sure that we have
500 feet separation above the crowd. Turning
right. I'm looking on the inside for Nos 4 and 8 to
make sure they've got plenty of room.
All join up into Swan."

Left: The Synchro Pair split away from the main formation to begin the second half of the display

Above: As the Synchro Pair describe the shape of a heart in the sky, the rest of the formation dive through in Seven Arrow. Against a blue sky the Team will use white smoke, if there is cloud, they use red

Spectacles and Opposition Barrel Roll from Synchro . . .

SYNCHRO

"As we get abeam threshold I call,
'TURN IN!'
Throttling back, hold 330 knots. I'm looking across at Synchro 2, making sure we are parallel, hold 330 knots, the main section has finished the Fan, I can see them clearing out of the corner of my eye, as we're coming round for the Inverted Spectacles. Quick check of Synchro 2's position around the turn and as we roll out along the line in front of the crowd, first man to threshold calls,
'THRESHOLD!'
It's me today and Synchro 2 isn't quite there so as he crosses he replies with,
'LATE!'
I come back on the power a bit to give him more time. But I can't take too much off or I won't have the speed for the manoeuvre: 300 knots minimum. We cross, not quite at datum. The wind is stronger than we thought. You spend all your life in Synchro fighting the wind, that's the big enemy. Just before the cross I call,
'ROLL, GO!'
'PUSH!'
As we roll on our backs we roll away from each other because that is the safe way. The jet tends to go the way you are rolling.
I know Synchro 2 will need to add two seconds to

his timing today so I call,
'PLUS 2!'
Check I've got $-3\frac{1}{2}g$ going up the hill, 2,400 feet, and at 2,500 feet,
'PULL!'
We both react together to my calls, that should keep us doing exactly the same thing at the same time. Up to 4,000 feet, adjusting power to reach 200 knots at 4,000 feet, and as we get there I call,
'4!'
As I pull through, Synchro 2 pauses, and puts in his allowance for wind. Thousand and one, thousand and two, and pulls through. I'm already going down the other side, but as he comes over with the wind he'll soon catch up. Coming down, looking at each other in the vertical, get the pitch angle just right. Approaching each other for the Opposition Barrel Roll, initially flying for a right to right cross; then just before we cross,
'ROLL, GO!'
Cross sides and do a barrel roll for a left to left cross, adjusting the pitch and roll to achieve a graceful roll with a punchy cross.
Bottoming the barrel roll at threshold, we turn crowd rear and I call,
'SYNCHRO CLEAR!'
This is as much for the boss to get his timing right as it is for Synchro 2."

then the main section come in with the Swan Roll . . .

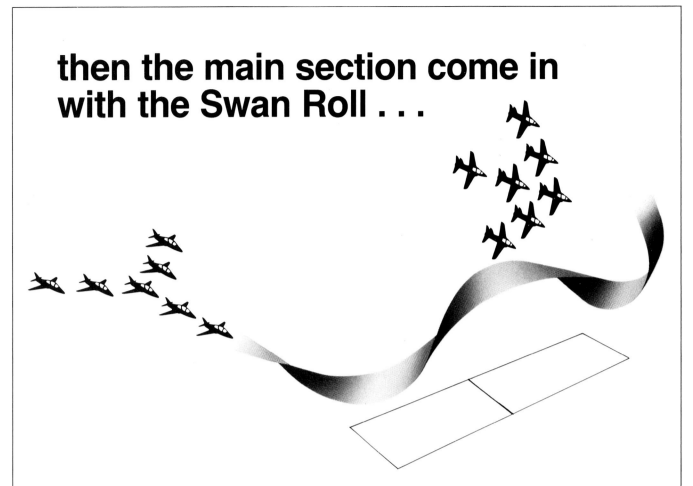

LEADER

"I have been watching Synchro and as they get towards threshold for the beginning of the Opposition Barrel Roll I call,
'MORE BANK, TIGHTENING!' and we pitch into the Swan Roll.
We're well on our way down as the solos do their Opposition Barrel Roll. They get to threshold and I listen for the Leader of the Synchros to call,
'SYNCHRO CLEAR!'
Then I call
'SMOKE ON, GO!'
'BANK COMING OFF A BIT!'
As soon as the solos are clear of threshold I call
'PULLING UP!'
25° of pitch, wings level,
'AND ROLLING!'
We start the Swan Roll and when we're upside down I call,
'THROTTLING BACK!' because we need to reduce speed for the next manoeuvre.
As we go crowd rear, I call,
'SEVEN ARROW, GO!'
'4! 5!'
Everyone switches smoke off automatically on that call and re-forms in Seven Arrow. The Synchro threshold call should come just as everyone switches their smoke off."

SYNCHRO

"The main section do the Swan Roll behind me so I can't see them. I've throttled back to 270 knots behind the crowd. Looking at Synchro 2, keeping parallel, hold 270 knots. Listening to the radio and as the boss calls,
'PULLING UP!', I call,
'TURN IN!' for the next manoeuvre.
Speed going up, setting full power 300, 320, 330 knots.
I'm looking across at Synchro 2 to make sure we reach threshold together by altering the rate of turn. As the boss is completing the Swan Roll, we are crossing threshold for the Boomerang."

Overleaf: The Synchro Pair pass each other at a relative speed of over 600 knots

Boomerang from the Synchro Pair . . .

LEADER

"I can see them coming underneath me as they come in for the Boomerang. We go out on a 45° to datum behind the crowd. As I come left,
'AIRBRAKES, GO!'
Round the corner, I'm looking for the solos. They should be inverted at 4,000 feet, coming in for the Boomerang."

SYNCHRO

"Approaching each other from thresholds, looking at Synchro 2 and at datum, trying to assess where the cross will occur.
Just before we cross I call,
'TURN!'
Both roll to 90° of bank. Hesitate for a moment to ensure a good cross, then snatch pull into a 6½g turn. Stop the turn at 45° going away from the crowd,
'ROLL, GO!'
270° roll and then,
'PULL, GO!'
Straight into another 6½g climb to 60° nose up.
At 1500 feet,
'ROLL, GO!'
And complete 1½ rolls. Check back on the stick to stop in the inverted position, aiming to top the manoeuvre at 4,000 feet, 200 knots and as we get there I call,
'4!'
At each call we do exactly the same thing to keep the manoeuvre symmetrical. At the top Synchro 2 puts the wind allowance in.
Over we go and coming down; looking for datum; looking at Synchro 2; he's looking at me; helping each other all the way; trying to get the cross exactly on datum; using full power or throttling back to idle if necessary.
The rule here is that as we cross, Synchro 2 always goes above and behind me. If he does get too far ahead and can't come back on power any more, he just calls, '6 BEHIND!' and if I acknowledge then it is up to me to miss him. If I don't say anything then he knows he's got to pull high and avoid me.
As we cross at datum Synchro 2 calls,
'CLEAR!'"

Left: The Team perform Roll Backs for the 300,000 people attending the
Air Day at USAF Ramstein in West Germany in 1986

Above: The Synchro Pair in a perfect cross

The Roll Backs . . .

LEADER

"As soon as I hear the call of '4!' I call,
'BIG SEVEN, GO!'
'4! 5!'
'2! 3!'
They all have to acknowledge because Nos 4 and 5 have to move out before Nos 2 and 3 can move in. If they miss the call, Nos 2 and 3 can't get in.
I can see Nos 2 and 3 come in either side of me. The solos are coming in to complete the Boomerang. Just before they cross I call,
'ROLLING OUT!'
After the 'CLEAR!' call from Synchro 2, I call,
'SMOKE ON, GO!'
I want about a 5 to 10 second run-in with the smoke on to allow the solos to re-position behind the crowd. I could get in much quicker but it makes it very difficult for them if I do.
As we cross the point where the Roll Backs should start I call,
'COLOUR ON, GO!'
'ROLL, GO!'
And Nos 2 and 3 pitch out, roll and as they come back into position behind me I hear,
'CLEAR!' from No. 2, and
'GO!' from No. 3; and Nos 4 and 5 pitch out.
They complete the manoeuvre and
'CLEAR!' comes from No. 4,
'GO!' from No. 5, and 8 and 9 pitch out.
There's not much for me to do here, just watch the solos to see how the timing is going, glance at the weather, lovely blue sky; we'll get the full show in today."

"Sometimes I have to cope with continuous changes from full to flat to rolling displays and back in one show. If you go into cloud just at the top of a loop or through a bit of thin cloud it is all right. But if we were to go into thick cloud it can be tricky. You don't want formation changes taking place in cloud. If it has to be a changing show it takes a lot of concentration. During the second half I also have to concentrate on the timing between myself and Synchro. Every site presents its own problems too. You have to find the points on the ground around which the display is orientated. If the conditions are difficult, ninety per cent of my concentration is on the weather and the rest should really be second nature. I should have in my own mind exactly what I'm looking for on the ground, but even display sites are sometimes difficult to see."

"At one display this season the weather was marginal so the crowd wasn't very big. There were times when the site disappeared completely. The visibility wasn't really so bad but the site was surrounded by cornfields and because of the dull weather, it didn't stand out at all. That was difficult, but generally we arrive and everything is just about in place. In the first couple of minutes I've seen all the points I'm looking for and after that I can concentrate on making absolutely certain that we're positioned correctly and I am flying smoothly. The harder I have to work, the harder the guys at the back have to work."

"Today the weather is lovely, so no problems there. Just as Nos 8 and 9 are coming back into their slots I can see Synchro coming towards datum. I can just see their smoke come on and I call,
'SMOKE OFF, GO!'
'COMING RIGHT, NOW!' "

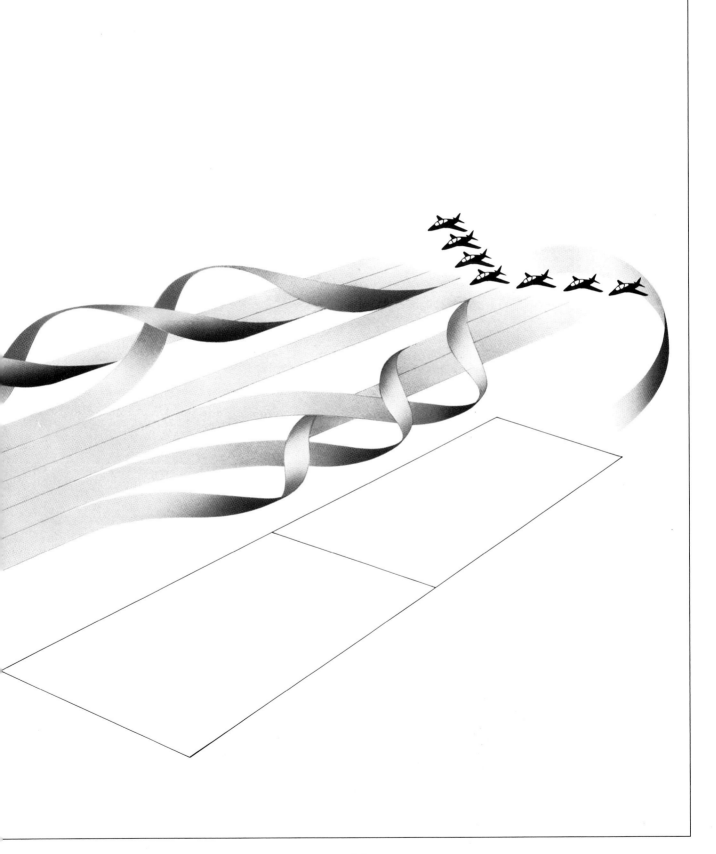

The Synchro Pair perform the Looping Carousel

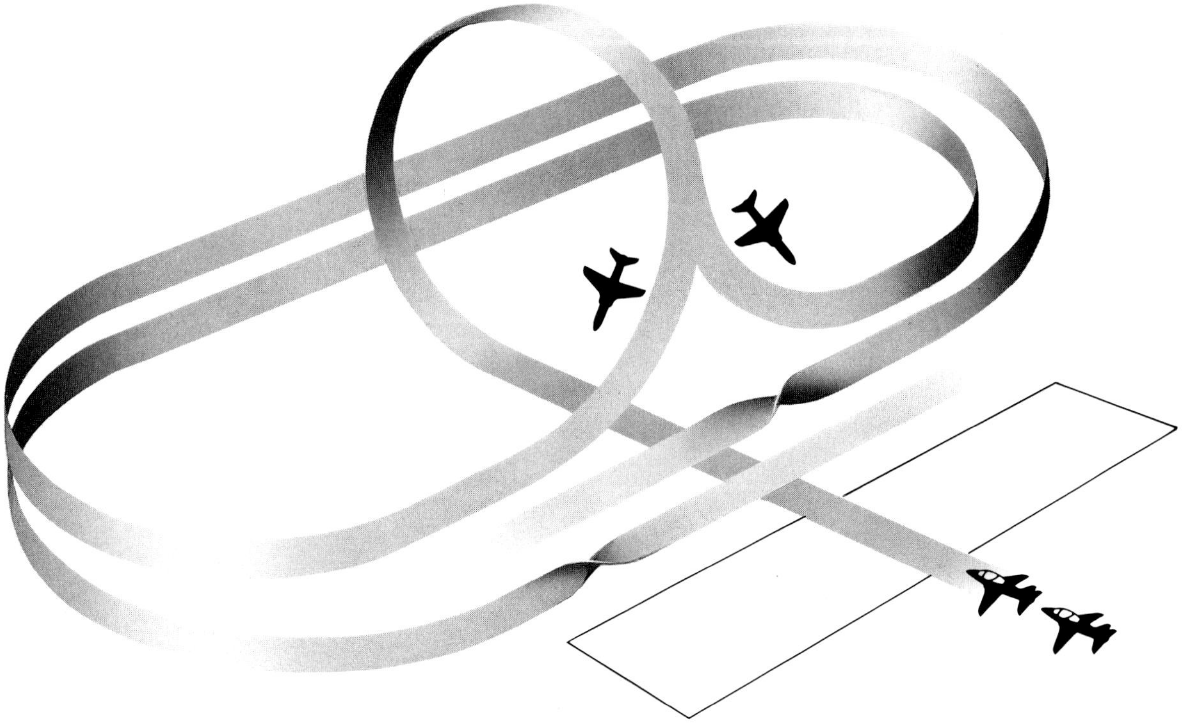

SYNCHRO

"While the main section is doing the Roll Backs, we go out round the back of the crowd. Synchro 2 is working very hard, trying to catch me to be in position for the Looping Carousel.

Running in, thinking about the wind, and assessing the position of the main section. I'm adjusting the turn to try and arrive as the Roll Backs finish. Looking at our shadows, I can see Synchro 2 in position behind me.

Approaching from crowd rear, pulling up, speed 330 knots, steady 4g.

I'm applying bank to keep the loop straight, float over the top, aiming for a minimum of 4,300 feet. As we descend and reach the vertical,

'SPLIT!'

Roll rapidly onto our respective 45° away from the crowd to begin the flat part of the Carousel."

Right: There is little room for error for the Synchro Pair but regulations require that the minimum separation between aircraft is 100 feet. For the crowd at right-angles to the display, they seem to fly straight at each other

LEADER

"As we come right, airbrakes go in, power comes on 2% to give us the speed we need for the next loop, then,

'ROLLING OUT!'

As I roll out I'm looking up and to my right to see how Synchro are doing. It's nice and tight and as the bank comes off I call,

'COMING LEFT, NOW!'

As I hear the solos call 'SPLIT!', I immediately call,

'SWAN, GO!'

'2! 3!'

And Nos 2 and 3 come in behind me as everyone else drops back."

SYNCHRO

"We split off, away from the crowd at 45°. At 1,200 feet I call,

'TURN IN!'

$4\frac{1}{2}g$ round the corner and cross on the far side, then continue the turn ensuring that the angle of bank and rate of turn remain constant.

Cross opposite datum in front of the crowd. Just after the cross,

'CLEAR!' from Synchro 2."

Caterpillar Loop . . .

LEADER
"Coming round the corner in Swan, I'm looking for the line to make sure I get lined up for the Caterpillar.

I'm looking in the mirrors to see that Nos 4 and 5 are settled and then call,
'LINE ASTERN, GO!'
'4! 5!'
Everyone else shuffles in numerically into a long line astern of seven aircraft. Then,
'ROLLING OUT!'
As I roll out, running down the runway, I'm watching the speed, 320 knots. Approaching the airfield, I see the solos complete the Carousel and I've heard them call 'CLEAR!'
There's one coming towards me, slightly low. He calls,
'SYNCHRO CLEAR!' and turns left in front of me. As he does that I call,
'SMOKE ON, GO!'
Front three put red on, middle one white and bottom three blue.
Speed increasingly slowly, 330, 340 and at the pull up point 350 knots.
As datum comes into my two o'clock I call,
'LEAD PULLING UP, NOW!' and I start the loop.
Gradually up to 3½g. Everyone is following me. As soon as I get upside down I call,
'THROTTLING BACK!' to prevent the back people becoming stretched. Everyone swaps their coloured smoke for white on that call.
Just past the vertical,
'LEAD COMING LEFT, NOW!'
Coming left and gradually, gradually feed the left bank on, letting it out slightly to make sure we bottom at 250 feet."

SYNCHRO
"Going away from the airfield behind the crowd.
'TURN REAR!'
Cross behind the crowd, passing datum, it looks about right, if not I'd make a correction. As the Leader calls 'THROTTLING BACK!' I call,
'TURN IN!'
The main section have just completed the Caterpillar Loop as we cross threshold for the Double Rolls and as we cross, I call,
'THRESHOLD!'
Looking at Synchro 2 and looking at datum."

LEADER

"Just as I'm coming to the bottom of that loop I hear the threshold call from Synchro and 'SMOKE OFF, GO!' from No. 9.

As the smoke goes off I can see all the aircraft coming up to join me in Big Seven on the left and right. Hold it for a moment, then as the power comes back on,

'COMING LEFT, NOW!'

I'm looking for Synchro to judge the timing for the next manoeuvre. They're coming round the corner, beginning to point towards datum."

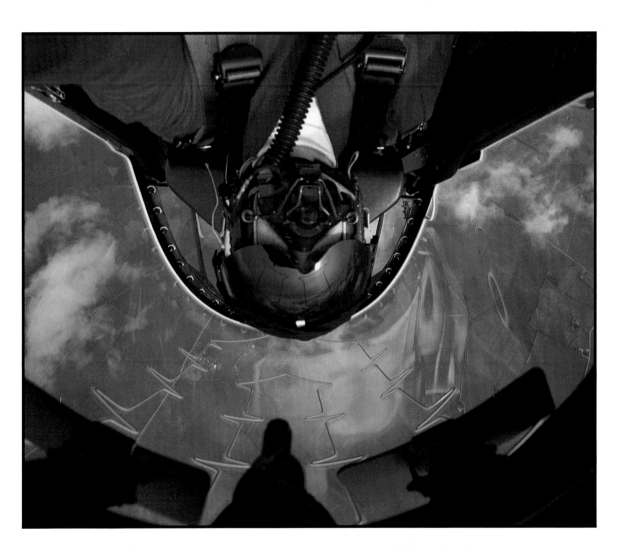

Left: Trailing red, white and blue smoke, the Hawks follow the Leader to
perform the Caterpillar Loop

Above: A new Red Arrows' pilot soon gets used to seeing the world
upside down

Front Cross and Derry Turn . . .

SYNCHRO

"I have a look to see how Synchro 2 is doing, ease back on the speed a touch, then,

'TURN!'

Maximum $6\frac{1}{2}g$ turn 45° away from the crowd. As we hit the 45°,

'ROLL, GO!' for a 270° roll under in a derry turn. Roll out, wings level, think about the wind. The boss is just coming round for the Box Loop and the Vixen Break.

'PULL, GO!' to 30° of pitch.

'ROLL, GO!' into another derry turn."

and . . . Double Rolls . . .

"Snatch to a maximum 6½g to turn crowd front
and arrive at thresholds. Just before threshold,
'PULL, GO!' into a high *g* barrel roll, to bottom
before datum.
'PULL, GO!' to achieve a cross with pitch up fol-
lowed by another barrel roll.
At threshold I call,
'SYNCHRO, CLEAR!' "

Overleaf: There doesn't always seem to be enough room in the sky for both
Synchro pilots at once!

Box Loop and the Vixen Break . . .

LEADER

"As Synchro get towards threshold and I call,
'SMOKE ON, GO!' I hear 'SYNCHRO CLEAR!'
and immediately I call,
'PULLING UP!'
Steady pull to 3½g again. Check the speed, check
the power and
'BOX, GO!'
'4! 5!'
Approaching the vertical, look left. In the vertical,
'VIXEN, GO!'
'4! 5!'
They go from line astern on me, to line astern on
Nos 2 and 3.
As we get upside down,
'THROTTLING BACK!' to prevent the speed
running away at the bottom of the loop.
Synchro call 'TURN IN!' for their next
manoeuvre. We come down, looking at datum,
getting the line exactly right. As we come down
towards the ground,
'LETTING IT OUT!' to get the Vixen Break right
in front of the crowd.
Gradually feeding off the g, coming up to the point
for the break,
'REDS, BREAK . . . BREAK . . . GO!'
On the second 'BREAK' I put my smoke on,
everyone else puts on their colour and on 'GO!'
everyone turns to their correct angle and pulls.
Pulling 7g so we get a nice explosive Break in front
of the crowd. As the Break is established,
'SMOKE OFF, GO!'
People on the outside reverse, pulling high to go
over the top of the crowd. I go right looking at No.
2 who is below me. He comes in to join me. I can't
see left because of the angle of bank. I roll out to 45°
going crowd rear, listening for Synchro coming in
for the Opposition Loop. Then,
'LEAD COMING LEFT, NOW!'
As we go left, I look for a point behind the crowd
line which will line me up at 90° to the crowd line."

Overleaf: The Synchro Pair's Opposition Loop is the hardest manoeuvre they do, and each winter they practise hard to ensure that there are no errors

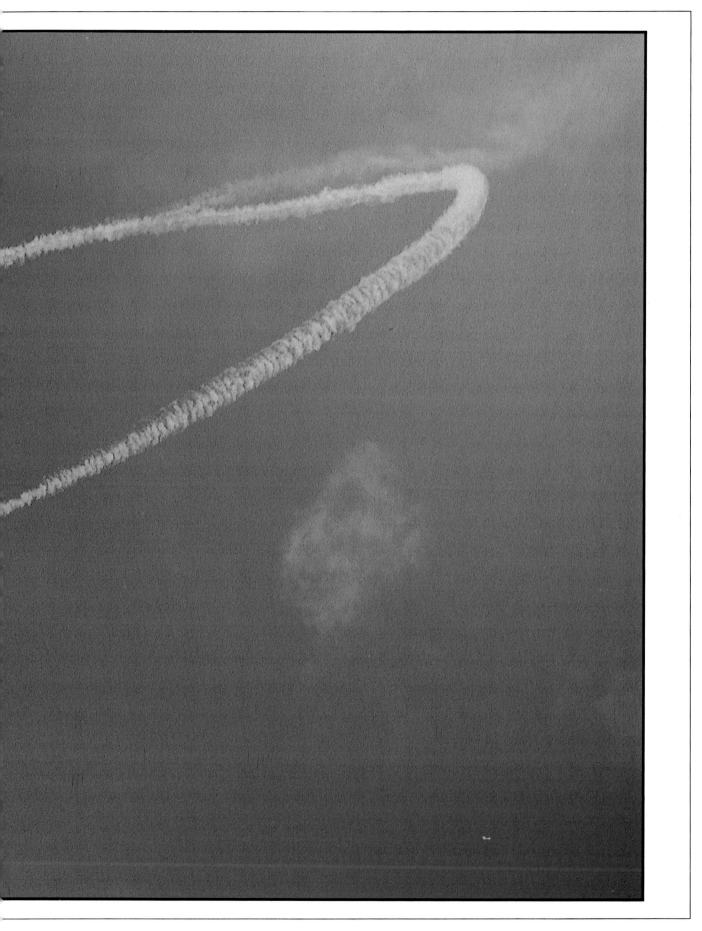

The Opposition Loop . . .

SYNCHRO

"As the Leader calls 'THROTTLING BACK!', I call,

'TURN IN!' for the Opposition Loop which is the hardest manoeuvre we do. It is the one time when I must think a long time ahead and get things exactly right from the start. I will never make a speed correction here, we need the speed to get the top cross in.

Passing threshold, final check for speed 330 knots.

'PULL, GO!'

To $6\frac{1}{2}g$ about 2,000 feet before the cross, aiming to cross with at least 30° pitch. Pulling a steady $6\frac{1}{2}g$, then at 60° of pitch, relax from $6\frac{1}{2}g$ to $2\frac{3}{4}g$.

In the vertical, looking backwards to catch the first sight of Synchro 2 coming towards me. I aim to top the loop at 4,000 feet.

As we cross, I can hear the sound of his jet so I know it's been a good one. As we descend I'm looking ahead for Synchro 2 to miss him in a right to right cross in front of the crowd.

Descend to 100 feet at threshold and call, 'SYNCHRO CLEAR!' "

LEADER

"We're coming in from crowd rear, looking for Synchro doing the Opposition Loop. They've finished the bottom cross and I hear 'SYNCHRO CLEAR!' I put my smoke on white just so they can see me. It can be quite difficult to see red aircraft against the ground."

SYNCHRO

"As we clear I go up to full power to ensure the speed for the hard 270° turn with maximum g up to $7\frac{1}{2}g$. Speed about 360 knots as I try and roll out abreast with the main section.

As soon as I see them I call, 'CONTACT!'

As I'm turning in alongside them, I'm belly up to the main formation so they are watching me. If I'm getting a bit close, they'll say 'STAY HIGH!' and I'll do that until I can see them, and then I'll drop into position."

Overleaf: The Parasol Break brings the show to a thrilling climax as the Hawks scatter in different directions

The Parasol Break

LEADER

"Round the corner I hear No. 6 say 'CONTACT!' and No. 7 calls '7!' which means they have both seen me so I switch the smoke off.
Then,
'ROLLING OUT!'
Coming from behind the crowd, datum just coming up,
'SMOKE ON, GO!'
I smoke red, everyone else smokes white.
Just after we're past datum,
'PULLING UP!'
As soon as the front four are together (Nos 1, 2, 3 and 4), No. 4 calls,
'SMOKE OFF, GO!' which only leaves the back five smoking.
At the top of the loop,
'6! 7!' which means they have joined up.
Just before the vertical coming down, I call,
'REDS, BREAK . . . BREAK . . . GO!'
On the second 'BREAK' everybody puts their smoke on. 'GO!' comes in the vertical and the Parasol Break opens up. I look left and right to see if the spacing is correct, then at 300 feet,
'PULLING UP!' and as soon as the nose starts coming up,
'SMOKE OFF, GO!' "

CHAPTER FOUR
THE PILOTS

The nine Red Arrows pilots are usually posted to the Team for only three years and in each season there are three new members. This ensures that the display is always fresh, with different ideas and personalities coming in every year. The pilots are ordinary serving RAF officers. They are paid the same as their contemporaries in other flying jobs and their time with the Red Arrows is simply another three-year posting. Nevertheless, every year there are far more men wishing to join than the three places available. Membership of the Team offers probably more flying and more fun than any other job in the RAF.

The pilots do generally feel that being in the Red Arrows is something of a sideways move in their RAF career. It is not a disadvantage to an officer to have flown with the Team, but it is no particular advantage either. The Red Arrows are a completely unique unit in the RAF, so being part of the Team does not automatically mean that the pilots are shown to be well suited to other roles in the Service. It can mean effectively putting their own careers in abeyance for three years – even though one of the Team's main roles is to encourage young men to take up careers in the RAF.

Despite this there are always volunteers waiting for the chance to go into the Team. The pilots are all men who put the enjoyment of flying high on their list of priorities. Rhodesian-born Flight Lieutenant Tony Lunnon-Wood joined the RAF through a special Commonwealth scheme, while he was living in New Zealand. Although he had not always wanted to fly, he knew his extrovert

---

Above: Squadron Leader Richard Thomas briefs the pilots before each take-off. Away from Scampton they will gather round the wing of Red 5's aeroplane

Right: Big Nine formation on a beautiful day

personality and dislike of routine needed a job that was both a challenge and offered constant variety. He opted for the RAF which in those days had bases all round the world and was flying many different types of aeroplane. In 1984 he joined the Red Arrows and the following year, to his great delight, was chosen to go into the Synchro Pair. He loved the flying, meeting new people and seeing different places, and felt the whole way of life suited him perfectly.

"It's totally enjoyable. For once in your life you are doing something that the public appreciate and you are working with a hand-picked bunch of blokes. It's a lovely three years doing something completely different."

There are usually thirty to forty applicants for the three vacancies that arise each year (two if a new Team Leader is also due to join the Team). A signal is sent out to all RAF stations asking for volunteers, and the pilots' applications, accompanied by both flying and character assessments from their superiors, arrive at RAF Scampton in January. The Commandant of CFS, the Station Commander, the Wing Commander and the Team Leader all receive copies of the applications. The Team Leader will then discuss the candidates with the rest of the Team and they decide on the short list.

At this stage probably the most important qualification a man can have is that he is known personally to some of the current Team. The Red Arrows are such a close-knit unit who have to work together constantly that they must choose men who will fit in well. As the RAF is a fairly small community, pilots of a similar age will usually have come across each other at some time.

Squadron Leader Richard Thomas, Team Leader from 1985–87, puts it quite simply, "We'll have met virtually everybody on that list. If they're not known it's really their fault. If you want to join you should try to make yourself known. It's very difficult to pick someone you've never seen before for this job – you choose the devil you know."

One of the ways the pilots ensure that they do become known is simply by applying several times. Flight Lieutenant Adrian Thurley joined the

Team for the 1986 season after his third application.

"It's fairly common to do that. If you don't know anybody on the Team you have got to apply anyway to get your name mentioned. I had been keen to do it almost as soon as I finished training. I had helped with the Team for a short time, while I was waiting to go to RAF Brawdy as a student and had flown with them in the back seat. I thought, this is for me.

"As soon as I finished my first tour, and completed 1,000 flying hours, which would be the absolute minimum requirements, I started applying. I knew that there was no way they would have taken me that first year.

"Then the next year, of course, I had only been at RAF Brawdy for twelve months, so I couldn't really expect to go then, but the following year I was due to leave Brawdy anyway in September. If I hadn't got in then, I wouldn't have applied again. Everything was right, I had done two full tours and, of course, by then I knew most of the Team. Charlie McIlroy who had joined the Team the previous year had been at Brawdy with me and was a close friend, although that is not necessarily an advantage. I have several good friends who I wouldn't have on the Team. I just don't think they could do the job and fit in. If you are right for the Team it certainly doesn't hurt to know someone well, if you are not right you wouldn't get in anyway."

The applicants for the 1987 season had applied to join the Team in January 1986. In April the seven short-listed pilots were invited to RAF Scampton for two days' flying and an interview, and to give the whole Team the chance of meeting them.

The men always spend their first morning flying with the Red Arrows. Short-listed candidates are among the very few people who are allowed to fly in all positions with the Team during their practices. They fly in the back seat of the Hawks behind the pilots to get an idea of what the display is actually like. Flight Lieutenant Spike Newbery, then a weapons instructor on Hawks at RAF Brawdy in Wales, was one of the men on the short list for the 1987 season:

"My first flight was totally exhilarating, absolutely magnificent. It really was unbelievable and quite different from what I expected. I hadn't done any formation aerobatics before and from the ground it all looks so tidy and neat. It seems perfectly smooth and yet when you are actually in the formation, especially down the back end, the aircraft are moving up and down, backwards and forwards all the time. I was very surprised and thought it must have looked awful, but then you see the video, and of course it looks fantastic. I then had a trip with Tony Lunnon-Wood in the Synchro Pair and that honestly was the most fantastic flying I've ever done, without doubt. Everybody who goes to the Red Arrows wants to fly Synchro."

The applicants usually have three flights on the first day and end by visiting a local pub with the pilots and some of the wives. Although Squadron Leader Thomas insists that "It's not to see if they slop their beer or anything like that," the evening does help the Team get to know all the candidates and assess whether or not they will fit in.

Any pilot who has got through to the short list will be capable of flying the display – Flight Lieutenant Newbery was surprised that the one thing no-one asked him to do was fly the aircraft, "But I suppose that would be unfair because I've flown in the Hawk a lot and some of the other guys are unfamiliar with it."

A pilot who is selected for the Team and has recently been flying different aircraft would be sent on a conversion course at RAF Valley before going to Scampton. The important thing for the short-listed candidates is whether or not they can become part of a closely-knit team.

During the display season the pilots are constantly together both in the air and on the ground and it is vital that disagreements are kept to a minimum.

"In the Team's history there have been personality clashes," says Squadron Leader Thomas. "It makes life very difficult indeed. It is important for the Team to be happy with the new members but you can never be certain. People can change. Sometimes, after two or three years, you realise you haven't got quite the right person, but it's too late once they're in, and you make the best of the situation. If they become too much of a problem you can of course always kick people out."

On the second day the candidates fly again with the Team in the morning and then have their formal interviews in the Commandant's office at CFS in the afternoon. The Commandant, the Station Commander, the Wing Commander and the Team Leader conduct the interviews which are, by this time, really a final filter.

Flight Lieutenant Newbery was one of the lucky ones. He heard very quickly that he had been selected and says:

"Although I knew joining the Red Arrows was not the best career move, I wanted to do some real pilots' flying; something that is great fun but also difficult and challenging. Once I knew I was in, it was difficult waiting from April to September to go to Scampton. It required a lot of effort to keep up my enthusiasm for the job I was doing although I was lucky in that weapons instructing is very demanding and very busy so I couldn't afford to sit back and wait."

The period between selection and joining the Team can be difficult for other reasons. The pilots all like to keep fit and enjoy sports and outdoor activities, but few of them want to risk breaking a leg skiing or playing football and be unable to fly.

Wing Commander Brian Hoskins was in the Red Arrows in 1975 and 1976 and then came back to lead the Team from 1979–81. He remembers how he felt before he rejoined them:

"It changes your attitude to a few things. The squadron I was on went to Norway on detachment and they decided to challenge the Norwegians to a game of soccer. They wanted me in the team as usual and so I played. But it was very very cold and the ground was frozen solid. I was getting a bit older and more prone to injury and I was afraid that if I got hurt I might not be able to lead the Team. In the end I just ran around looking busy but didn't actually lunge into any tackles – and our goalkeeper did in fact break his leg during the match."

The new pilots join the Team in the September

Left: A pilot's-eye view of a Red Arrows display

Top: Flight Lieutenant Charlie McIlroy prepares to strap in

Above: A five/four cross performed in earlier display seasons

in time to fly in the back seats during the last month of the display season. This is when they really get their first chance to see how the Red Arrows operate. They begin to experience the reality of working through weekends, and as they travel to air shows around the country and abroad, they get their first taste of the public's keen interest. The Red Arrows have a very faithful following who are constantly eager to collect the autographs of their heroes. One thing the new recruits do notice is that to the public the Team is everything. The fact that the personnel change each year matters not at all. The only criterion is to be in the Red Arrows – and to wear a red flying suit. Until they fly as pilots in the Team, the new members have to make do with RAF regulation green and are largely ignored by voracious autograph hunters. It is an early lesson and one which they will remember when the time comes to leave.

Flight Lieutenant Pete Collins joined the Team in September 1985. He vividly remembers his month in the back seat of the jets.

"The red suit opens just about any door. The pilots are welcomed everywhere – and then there are the three new guys and no one is quite sure who they are. But the red suit only lasts three years so you have to make the most of it."

When Pete Collins first went to Scampton he soon became known as a practical joker, and it was not long before one victim decided to get his revenge. While Pete was still flying as a passenger, experiencing displays and life on the road, he was suddenly told that it was usual practice for the future Team members to sit in the *front* of the Hawk and fly one display under instruction from the Red Arrows pilot sitting behind.

"I wasn't sure if he really meant it and if he did, I thought I'd look an idiot if I refused, so I got in the front." Pete Collins then had to sweat it out until the last moment before start-up when he was let off the hook and allowed to retreat to the back seat.

It seems that one of the qualifications for a Red Arrows pilot is being able to take a joke. During their first couple of months with the Team they are especially vulnerable. Flight Lieutenant Spike

Newbery was very worried when a member of the public watching outside the airfield at RAF Scampton apparently complained that his car had been ruined by the dye in the smoke he had used at low level. Spike had only been with the Team for a couple of weeks and was flying on his own, practising aerobatics when, like every new Team member, he could not resist trying out the smoke. The angry northerner rang up the crew room and spoke "by chance" to the hapless pilot.

He would not calm down, saying that not only was the car covered with dye, but that his wife who had a weak heart, had hardly been able to breathe. He threatened to take the matter further, and Spike had to tell the Team Leader what had happened and to expect trouble – not a good beginning to his new job. The other pilots turned the screw, saying that he had ruined the goodwill they had built up over years and Flight Lieutenant Newbery began to feel that his Red Arrows career might be over before it had started. He was eventually summoned to face the irate northerner, who he could hear complaining loudly as he approached the Team Leader's office, only to discover that he was in fact Flight Lieutenant Pete Lees, one of his fellow pilots. Spike soon realised that the whole Team, including the Leader, were in on the joke – he had been well and truly set-up.

Flight Lieutenant Dan Findlay joined the Red Arrows for the 1986 season. Like Spike Newbery he had been a weapons instructor on Hawks at RAF Brawdy and while there he flew solo aerobatics in the Hawk for a display season. This confirmed a growing feeling that he would like to join the Team.

"The flying is fantastic and you are working with guys who all get on well together. It's part of the selection procedure that the guys in the Team want you, so it is a unique working environment. The other great thing is that we are doing a job that the public appreciate. Normally as a fighter pilot you spend your time training for something you hope you will never have to do for real. This job is fantastic. You train for six months to do something throughout the summer that the public love. It's very satisfying. The Red Arrows really is a one-off job in the Service. Guys who get selected for the Team certainly have the potential to do quite well in the Force, but first and foremost they really do enjoy flying."

Squadron Leader Thomas agrees: "It attracts people who are more interested in flying than in the career. It's difficult because people arrive on the Team when they really should be in an executive post. They've been in the Air Force for some time and are quite experienced. The trouble is that they come to the Team and you really can't assess their organisational and supervisory abilities because they just don't get that experience here. As far as they and the RAF are concerned, they are marking time and when they leave they can be three years behind everyone else.

"Even as Leader I am marking time, because I've done my Flight Commander tour and I've been written up and assessed on that. It was a flying supervisor job and you don't generally get two Squadron Leader flying tours. When I finished that tour and if I was following the ideal path, I would have been selected for Staff College, then done a ground tour, been promoted and returned as a squadron boss. That is the ideal progression for a career officer but as it turned out, I came here instead. I'm a squadron boss here, but it's not front line and that is what the RAF is really about.

"This job is quite different from a normal supervisory job. I brief and lead everything so I'm much more in a position where I can make mistakes. On a squadron you generally don't lead a great deal because you are always assessing other people. Because the turnover is so fast you often fly in formations right down the back, assessing new pilots. You very seldom have to go out in front and show them how it's done. In this job, of course, it's entirely different. In the broadest terms I'm here to lead the nine aircraft around the sky and promote the Team. I'm responsible for all three branches of the squadron: operational, administrative and engineering.

"If we didn't turn up at a display site or arrived at the wrong time because the organisation was incorrect, it would be my responsibility – although the administrative side would have some questions to answer.

"I'll finish this tour having spent nearly four years out of the front line, still not having been to Staff College, still not having done a ground tour – all things the RAF considers to be important – and end up having to catch up.

"Having said that, we all enjoy the life and we all enjoy the flying and we get the opportunity to see life from two different sides. We meet a lot of people from civilian life as well as those in the Service, so we are in a good position to make a balanced judgement on what life is like outside. We talk to lots of people but we should be under no illusions. Life in the RAF *is* very secure."

As soon as the season ends most of the Team go off for two weeks' holiday, leaving the Team Leader (referred to as "the boss") and the three new pilots. They will spend a week following him around the skies practising aerobatics. The new pilots already know in which position they will fly and from the beginning they always practise on one specific side of the diamond shape.

They do ten sequences of formation aerobatics at 3,000 feet, then ten at 1,000 and fifteen at 500 feet. This takes place in the two weeks while the rest of the Team are away – the boss has the second week off, leaving the new pilots in the hands of his Deputy Leader. The new pilots usually fly in positions 4, 5, 8 or 9, on the outside or at the back of the formation. In some ways these are the most difficult positions to fly and certainly provide the most uncomfortable ride, but the Team have found that it is important to have a stable platform at the front on which the rest of the Team can formate. The Leader, together with Nos 2, 3 and 6 (Synchro Lead) form an experienced solid diamond and the new pilots can perfect their own positions without affecting anyone else.

One of the first things each new pilot has to do in addition to the flying is study the Red Arrows' Standard Operating Procedure (the SOP). This is a weighty document, detailing exactly how the Red Arrows must operate. It contains all the rules and

Left: The Team make the formations and manoeuvres look so easy but each one takes hours of practice. Here, during a training session, they attempted to loop Concorde, but found that the aircraft at the back didn't have the power to hang on

Above: The 1986 Synchro Pair, Tony Lunnon-Wood and Charlie McIlroy, discuss their part of the show

regulations governing the Team including training, the procedure for briefings, the use of unmodified aircraft during practices and what to do in each specific emergency. It gives diagrams and information about the current display, going into great detail. On a manoeuvre like the Vixen Break, it lays down exactly which aircraft go where. Copies are kept in the Briefing Room and the pilots all have to sign as having read them. They must know the SOP inside out, as they will be tested annually when the examiners (the "trappers") appear. As one pilot said, "It gives all our secrets away. It's quite simple really: pull the stick back and the cows get smaller!"

When the whole Team return from leave, they begin to build up the display. Initially the Leader and the Synchro Pair, who fly directly behind him, will fly with the three aircraft from one side of the diamond formation then do the same with the three aircraft from the other side. This is known as flying "sides" and allows all the pilots to get used to their new positions and ensure that the formations are perfect. The Synchro Pair will also go off together while the other aircraft practise their own manoeuvres.

The new pilots must learn to use one specific reference point to keep the formations exact. In Diamond 9, for example, Nos 2, 3, 6, 8 and 9 formate directly on the Leader. No. 7 flies behind No. 6, and Nos 4 and 5 on the outside line up the heads of Nos 2 and 1, or Nos 3 and 1, respectively. They look for only one reference and do not try to look across the formation at the same time. As far as possible they formate only with the Leader, eliminating the whiplash effect that would occur if they formated on a pilot in between, who might be moving up and down in turbulence, trying to maintain his own position. When they watch the video they can tell how precise they have been and then, when they begin flying the complete formation, they can correct any mismatch between the sides.

Adrian Thurley remembers his first winter training very clearly: "Once you get over the initial hurdle of wondering whether you can manage the flying, it becomes great fun. To begin with you really have to work hard to remember exactly what to do. When the Leader calls for a formation change, you acknowledge before you move, but if you can't quite think what your move is, then you say nothing.

"It doesn't happen often but if the boss didn't hear any acknowledgement, he would know that you had a problem and would run through the move. So you hear the call, know what you are going to do, acknowledge and then do it. That way everyone knows that you have heard the call and are about to move."

Spike Newbery, having recovered from his initiation into the Team, really enjoyed his early weeks of formation practice. "I haven't yet come back from a trip where I haven't been smiling, even if I've not been particularly happy with my own performance. It is just such good fun. You settle into formation aerobatics quite quickly. You get there or thereabouts but then perfection takes a long time. We do have some very honest de-briefs after the sorties. If anything, I expect we are a bit hard on ourselves but that is probably a good thing at this stage.

"I am flying as Red 4, on the outside of the formation. It is one of the more difficult positions, especially in the Wineglass Roll when I am on the end of a straight line, and in Viggen when I fly at the back. It can be very bumpy. In Wineglass you line up heads to get the line straight but having done that, you also have to get the spacing between the aircraft correct. I don't know why but you soon get a feel for the way it should be. I had done formation flying and I'd done aerobatic flying before, but until I joined the Team I hadn't done the two together. It's obviously not impossible or we wouldn't be doing it, but it is difficult to make it look perfect.

"You have to get used to the rates of roll to begin with, although the boss is very consistent and I already know how fast he will pull. It is really all constant practice and discussion.

"Acknowledging the boss's calls is one of the most difficult things to get right at first. You must acknowledge in a specific sequence so that everyone knows that everyone else is aware of exactly what is going on. In the beginning we got it wrong a few times, but if that happens you just stay put until the boss sorts it out. Unless everybody hears the correct sequence of acknowledgements, nobody moves.''

Just like the rest of the Team, the Synchro Pair changes every season. Each year it is made up of a pilot in his third year who will lead the pair and a pilot in his second year who will then lead in his third year. Flight Lieutenant Charlie McIlroy, the only bachelor of the 1986 team, was Synchro 2 in that year. It also took him three attempts to get in to the Team but he was greatly helped on the third try by having just flown the Hawk solo display for a season.

"I really wanted to get in. Display flying, whether you're in the Team or doing solo stuff, is really good fun because you are flying the aeroplane to the absolute limits and close to the ground which is very exciting. It is a great challenge because you are being watched, either by a bunch of discerning pilots or by 50,000 people at an air show and you want to get it exactly right. If you come down and you know that you've done a really good display, it makes you feel very good.

"When I first joined the Team I went into the No. 8 slot. That was very different from the solo aerobatics I had been doing. Your view of the world is looking at the boss and occasionally at one of the other aeroplanes. I didn't find it terribly difficult to do the flying but I found it difficult to do it really well. But it was fantastic, one hundred per cent tremendous and far far better than I had imagined it would be. Not only the flying, but the whole way of life. You are working with eight other guys who are incredibly enthusiastic and are professionals as well. I wanted to fly Synchro from the beginning because that would involve me in a little bit of formation flying with the Team at the start of the display and then in the second half you can really let go."

Charlie McIlroy was born in Belfast. He learnt to fly there on a flying scholarship with the Air Training Corps and then joined the RAF when he had completed his 'A' levels. He will happily tell people about his inability to organise himself and what stupid things he can do on the ground – but, like all the Red Arrows, is far more reticent about his flying skills. He is, in fact, often described as a natural pilot, a man more at home in the cockpit of his aircraft than under the bonnet of his car. No-one was surprised when Charlie was picked to go into the Synchro Pair, least of all Squadron Leader Al Chubb who was the only other candidate that year.

"I did have a hankering to fly Synchro when I joined but I would have had to break both Charlie's legs and put him in hospital to get it! He really is ideally suited."

Flight Lieutenant Tony Lunnon-Wood was flying as Leader of the Synchro Pair when Charlie joined him as his No. 2.

"In the beginning we sat down with the boss and chatted about what we wanted to do, if it was feasible and how we were going to blend it in with the rest of the display. Then I went and practised on my own. Synchro 2 has to fly in stages anyway, working down to be cleared for 100 feet. The rest of the Team are only cleared to 250 feet. He needs about three weeks by himself before he can do any synchro at all. For a year he has been doing nothing but follow the boss around and now he's got to start flying the jet to its limits.

"When he's ready we start off and do timing runs. I fly off down one side of the runway, Synchro 2 knows where I will be and I say, you put yourself there, have a look at it, fly past me and as you get more comfortable we'll move the distance in. We'll do that for a couple of trips until he is happy. You get used to it quite quickly. Then we'll start doing manoeuvres. We start off with the Opposition Barrel Roll and do nothing but a sortie of them. When that is right we'll go up and try the Boomerang. It's just the simple manoeuvres first. We normally save the Opposition Loop till last and really psych ourselves up for that one. Then we'll do nothing but Opposition Loops for a couple of days and finally put the whole package together.

"The Opposition Loop is without doubt the

Overleaf: Flight Lieutenant Tony Lunnon-Wood, Synchro Lead in 1986, prepares for a transit flight. His ground crew "back seater" is behind him

most difficult manoeuvre we do. There is a lot of room for error in it. On all the other manoeuvres you are normally travelling at around 300 to 330 knots, so you have speed to play with and if things are going wrong at any stage, if I don't like the way the cross is going, I can pull away from Charlie or he can push away from me and we have lots of response.

"With the Opposition Loop the first cross is simple but for the top cross you are at a very low speed and don't have the same control over the aircraft. You have to have the loop set up a long way in advance and you have to make a very early decision if things are going wrong. If, in an emergency, I didn't like it or if things didn't seem right, we'd actually call the manoeuvre off, roll it out and disappear crowd rear, letting the spectators focus on the boss. This is the one manoeuvre where we'll never make a speed correction to ensure that the cross is exactly at datum.

"Once we hit threshold, we accept the speed and if it goes down wind or up wind, you just forget it because you must have the speed to get the height and get the top cross in. The Opposition Loop is something you go through very carefully in the winter training and you think about it long and hard beforehand. As long as you make an early decision, there is no problem.

"The thing you must *never* do in Synchro is say 'I'll get this right if it kills me.' What you do say is: 'If in doubt, take the simple way out.' You never ever try and press on and get it right at all costs. After a while you get a feel for just how far to go on trying. But the golden rule is, always a comfortable missed distance for both of you, not just for one of you, for both of you. And, of course, safety for the crowd.

"Everybody, unless they are a liar, frightens themselves at some stage during the winter work-up. But there's no point in trying to impress anybody. I said to Charlie, 'I've got a wife and kids, you've got a girlfriend, you might kill yourself trying to get a cross in, and what's it worth?' Half the crowd wouldn't know anyway because it is all aimed at datum and there are only about 50 people either side of that who would see exactly where we cross, the rest of them haven't got a clue.

"You've got to have a really dependable Rock of Gibraltar for Synchro 2, someone you know is not going to do anything scatty or unexpected. It's very easy to get carried away and to try very hard to get it right all the time. There are occasions when you can't do it and you have just got to accept that and say: 'It wasn't a good show, we're sorry, but we know why.' If you know the reasons why, you are happy. If you don't know, that's when you've got a problem.

"You need a guy who has got the courage of his convictions in the bar, when people are saying, 'Hey, you had the crosses 200 metres out today!' He must be able to say: 'Yes, well, you try it mate if you think you could do any better.' He's got to just let it go over him and not think, 'OK, tomorrow, I'm really going to get it right' – that's when you end up killing each other.

"But it is very easy to get carried away by the crowd. It is a big discipline and that is why I'm not at all keen to have youngsters on the Team. As a youngster you could very easily get carried away with the occasion and put yourself in situations where you can't recover. All you do is let the Team down and hurt the public and your family. All you've done is bad and aviators are very unforgiving if you make a mistake. It's a very hard school.

"So you must take it in gentle stages and as you are happy with one manoeuvre, then you go on to the next and you never go faster than the new guy can manage. After a while you should get a mental telepathy going, and although it is Synchro Lead's job to try and get all the crosses on the line, sometimes Synchro 2 can see things building up and help out. You need a bit of chemistry – if you didn't get on particularly well with the bloke it just wouldn't work."

The Synchro Pair exist very much as a team within a team. Because of the constant high g turns they pull, they are the only pilots who wear an anti-g suit. This is a laced green corset, which they wear over their flying suits and which is plugged into the aeroplane. As the aircraft pulls g, the suits inflate, squeezing the muscles in the legs and abdomen, which prevents blood from draining from their heads. This stops them blacking out as the aircraft go into violent high-*g* turns.

The rest of the Team also pull a lot of *g* on manoeuvres like the Vixen Break and the Parasol Break, but it only lasts for a few seconds and they prefer to fly the display without the restriction of the *g*-suit.

Before each trip the Synchro Pair get together to brief the flight, discuss the conditions and talk through any problems they have. When they have done this they will then join the rest of the Team for the briefing from the Leader.

At RAF Scampton this takes place next to the Crew Room, in the Briefing Room. This is where displays are discussed and manoeuvres planned. At the front there is a large white board on which there are nine magnetic red shapes of the Hawk, each marked with a different number. These are used during training to illustrate the formations and to show how each aircraft must move during the changes. A large glass wall cabinet covers diagrams of the sequence of formations for the current season's full display – another contains the manoeuvres and formations used during rolling shows and flat shows. The video recorder and television are also kept in the Briefing Room and the pilots watch each display and practice to see exactly how the formations and changes are going.

Before each sortie the Team Leader will give the pilots details of weather conditions and discuss exactly what they are going to do. If they are going away he will tell them about the route and any hazards to watch out for, the location of nearby airfields in case any of them have to divert, and anything else they must know.

The pilots go into the briefing from the Crew Room but as soon as it is finished they usually head straight out for their aeroplanes – or "walk" as it is called – through another door. The briefing must be completely fresh in their minds, there is no time for a last cup of coffee and a chat.

In addition to the normal winter training the pilots have to keep up the flying skills which they would not normally use during the display season. During the winter in his second year Flight Lieutenant Lunnon-Wood experienced the most common major problem faced by the pilots.

"I had gone up to do a navigation exercise and had a navigator friend in the back who had just come for the ride. It was early evening and there were a lot of birds around. We were at 500 feet and about to start a target run and I had just looked down at a map when the guy in the back said 'Birds!' I just managed to poke the nose of the aeroplane down an inch or two when a bird went straight through the top of the canopy, straight behind my right shoulder and into my seat. It was very noisy and there were lots of glass and bits flying around. I was separated from the guy in the back by the blast screen and when the bird hit my seat it vaporised into blood all over the screen and he couldn't see what had happened. He thought it was my blood!

"Because of all the noise, we couldn't talk on the radio although apparently he was shouting at me to see if I was okay and to find out whether he should jump out. I was madly giving hand signals, not realising that he couldn't see anything.

"The jet was flying straight and level and I thought if I kept it pointing away from the ground he would know we were all right. We finally got back in contact and I convinced him that I wasn't dead.

"It wasn't too difficult to fly although it was very noisy. Once you have established that the engine is still going, a great load goes off your shoulders and you have time to think. We diverted into the nearest airfield and it was lucky I had someone with me. Some of the glass had richocheted off me and hit the air-speed indicator and it had seized solid. The chap behind me read out the air speeds from his instruments and we landed without too much trouble. It was just very noisy and very windy."

It is surprising how much harm one small bird can do. Bird strikes are the most common cause of damage to aeroplanes, although sometimes a bird will go straight through an engine and emerge the

Overleaf: High above the English countryside, the Red Arrows loop in Diamond Nine formation

other side without causing any problems – to the aeroplane. Minor strikes can simply dent the outer skin of the fuselage, but birds can also cause so much damage that an aircraft has to be virtually rebuilt and is out of service for months.

Charlie McIlroy thought he was particularly unlucky with birds. By the end of his second year with the Team, he had suffered a total of fifteen bird strikes since he began flying Hawks (although most were not with the Red Arrows). These ranged from the time when he hit a seagull and could find no damage at all, to the time when he had a multiple strike from a flock of high soaring crows, which resulted in the aeroplane being unserviceable for fourteen months.

During the winter when the pilots are practising in different combinations and all the aircraft have to undergo a thorough servicing – the deep winter strip – there will be only five or six aeroplanes available for the Team each day, but by the middle of January each year the aircraft must be ready to take on their full work load. Around this time, the pilots will fly the first "nine-ship" and put the whole display sequence together. It is a big leap forward and from then on they always practise together and really start to become a team.

Because of the vagaries of the English weather, much of their practice is taken up with flat and rolling displays – the Red Arrows' answer to low cloud base and poor visibility. In order to ensure that the Team are also able to bring the full spectacular display up to standard, the pilots and ground crew go off to Cyprus on detachment for three weeks in April. There the display can be perfected in the (usually) fine weather of the Mediterranean.

"It's the time to put the icing on the cake really," says Dan Findlay. "At RAF Scampton in the winter we don't get the chance to do that many full displays so we go to Cyprus and do them three times a day, day after day."

By the end of the three weeks the display is perfected and the Team are ready to return to England. Before they can leave for the UK, however, they must have the approval of the Commander-in-Chief, Support Command. Before he takes his

look at the display other people in the chain of command will have watched and given their approval, but it is the C-in-C's final clearance which allows the Team to "go public".

Each year the first official public Red Arrows display is held on "Families Day" at the end of the detachment in Cyprus. The pilots wear their red flying suits for the first time that year and it marks the start of their display season. When they leave Cyprus to return to England, some of the pilots think that the display is at its best. They have just experienced two or three weeks of consistent practice in perfect weather – and the English summer to come will probably not give them such an opportunity again. From now on they quickly get into the routine which will continue all season. They work virtually every weekend and usually have two days off during the week to compensate.

Squadron Leader Richard Thomas soon found that, for the Leader, days off were extremely rare and that the job was very different from the time when he was an ordinary member of the team. He had first joined the Red Arrows in 1976:

"I had been stationed at RAF Kemble, on the Gnat training squadron which used to be co-located with the Red Arrows there. I finished the course I was doing in February 1976 and I was going to apply to join the Team. Then one of them had a car accident and they didn't know how soon he would be fit. As they already knew me they asked if I'd mind standing in for a while. In fact the guy recovered very quickly and the weather was awful so in the three weeks I was there I only flew a couple of times. However, I'd got my foot in the door so I immediately put in an application and got picked at the end of April 1976.

"I went to RAF Valley and did six months instructing while I waited to join the Team and then went to Kemble in September 1976. I stayed for four years and flew No. 8 in the first year and then did one year as No. 2 of the Synchro, then two years as Synchro Lead. It was an interesting period, of course, because we had the changeover from Gnats to the new Hawks.

"The Hawk in essence is a very simple aircraft

to fly. In operational terms it is simpler than the Gnat. The Gnat, once you were airborne, was a very nice aircraft to fly. On the ground, however, the landing speeds were a good 20 knots faster than the Hawk and so ground handling was not so easy. It was more susceptible to cross winds.

"The most obvious difference, however, was the feel and the handling of it. The Gnat performed like a swept wing aircraft and we were all used to swept wing aircraft, where if you got into trouble and wanted more lift, you kept pulling back on the stick and the aircraft turn-rate would increase. The Hawk is very much a straight winged aircraft so the technique is different. If you do get into trouble and need more lift out of the wing, if you keep pulling you eventually get to the stage where the wing just stalls and you don't turn at all. That was the most obvious difference, particularly in Synchro.

"After the Gnat season ended in 1979, we did our conversion course, a basic four or five trips at Valley, before we came back to Kemble again to start practising for the display as usual. We started Synchro practice with very, very few hours on the aircraft, in my case after ten sorties on the Hawk which constituted about 13 hours flying. It was quite interesting, especially initially.

"Obviously there were areas about which we were concerned. We had to look closely at looping heights. When we started off, everyone said the Hawk turns better than the Gnat but it became apparent that, at the speeds we used, we could do a much tighter display in the Gnat than we could in the Hawk. So we started raising the heights at the top of manoeuvres. Now we are usually 1,000 feet higher on the individual loops than we were with the Gnat. That's a lot of height."

Wing Commander Hoskins, now working in the Ministry of Defence and doing his first desk job after twenty-two years' flying, was leading the Team during the changeover from Gnats to Hawks:

"It was very interesting because we were the first Red Arrows pilots to fly Hawks. They had been in service about three years and there was a lot of expertise on the aeroplane; but there were major differences between the two aircraft and we were the first to experience them in the Team.

"The Hawk accelerates and decelerates slower than the Gnat. The Gnat used to respond more like a propeller engine and as soon as you touched the power you got a response. With the Hawk we didn't get the instant response we were used to. You had to keep the rpm as high as you could; if you came back on the power too much, the problems of acceleration were even greater. The Hawk is also a much bigger aeroplane so there is more inertia. If you were flying in No. 4 or 5 position you were in a much bigger arc and the radius of the rolls was much greater, which meant more power changes. It wasn't really more difficult but it was very different and it took time to come to terms with the differences.

"To make it easier, of course, we had brand-new fully serviceable aeroplanes and they were all available for us to use from 1st October. Normally the Team would only have five or six aeroplanes at the start of the winter training, because of the servicing schedule, but in 1979 we were operating with ten aeroplanes from the beginning.

"It was also the first year in which we went off to Cyprus on detachment before the beginning of the season. This has now become the norm and it does take a great load off the Team, knowing that at the end of the training season there will definitely be two weeks' fine weather in which to practise.

"The only other concession to the new aeroplanes was that we decided to keep the Synchro Pair together. I thought that their task would be the most difficult and they needed to be very experienced. They had a lot to learn with the Hawks. The handling differences between the two aeroplanes were, of course, something the Team only had to come to terms with during the first year. By the second and third year, we had the expertise to pass on to the new pilots."

During the first display season with the Hawk, the lower flying limits were changed, though not because of any difficulties with the new aeroplane. Richard Thomas was leading the Synchro Pair:

"We were supposed to be flying at 50 feet then,

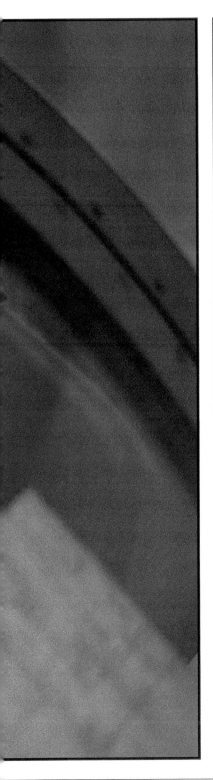

Left: Brian Hoskins led the Team from 1979 to 1981 during the changeover from the Gnats to the new British Aerospace Hawk

Above: The Crew Room at RAF Kemble before the Team moved to Scampton. Facing the camera is Squadron Leader Tim Miller, due to rejoin and lead the Team for the 1988 to 1990 seasons

with a 'not below' limit of 35 feet. After Brighton it went up to 100 feet and it's been 100 feet ever since. At Brighton we were displaying over the seafront when a boat suddenly motored across underneath us. Steve Johnson, flying Synchro 2, was coming the other way to me and he hit the mast just before we crossed. I didn't see it happen and I continued to fly down the line, turned right and looked back. There was no aircraft, nothing. Sometimes you can't see your No. 2 so I thought, maybe he's gone straight on for some reason. I carried on until I heard the Manager say that he'd ejected, so obviously it was time to call it a day. Unfortunately we couldn't continue to operate at those heights afterwards."

Wing Commander Hoskins, leading the main formation, remembers the day very clearly:

"I heard the Synchro call for their manoeuvre and I started to position the Team for ours. Then I heard the Manager say that one of the Synchros had hit an aerial. I said, 'Are you sure?' because I knew they were over the sea and as we completed our manoeuvre he said, 'He's ejected and I can see him in the water.' I stopped the display and told Richard Thomas to stay there, putting out a mayday call, until Synchro 2 was picked up. We were halfway back to Biggin Hill, our display base, when I heard he had been picked up by boat."

Steve Johnson was uninjured and was taken back by helicopter to join the Team at Biggin Hill within hours.

"The ejection seat was close to its limits but it worked exactly as it should," says Brian Hoskins. "His decision needed to be quick and it was, but he had no problems at all from the seat. In fact we were back at Biggin Hill, briefing to do the 8-ship display that afternoon, when he landed in the helicopter and walked across to us. I said, 'Okay Steve? Come and join the briefing, we've got the spare aeroplane.' Of course I didn't mean it, but he said, 'Yes, okay boss!' He was fit enough to fly although it obviously wouldn't have been the right thing to do. In fact he had the usual medical checks and was back flying after a few days."

"All the Synchro heights were jacked up after that," says Squadron Leader Thomas. "You feel you've let people down really. You've been given authority to fly at very low heights. Since then the Synchro Pair has to fly higher and we'll never get back to those heights again. The heights we fly at now are reasonable, not too low and not too high. Most people can see us. It's not as demanding flying at these heights as flying at 35 feet, although it's very hard work doing it at any height. You've still got to get it absolutely right. You can't make a mistake."

When Richard Thomas left the Red Arrows in 1980 he was posted to an RAF base in West Germany to a front line squadron, flying Harriers. Like most pilots, he loved flying the vertical take-off aeroplane but because of the Falklands conflict, he spent a lot of time away from home. Heather, his wife, refers to this as her "unaccompanied tour". Contrary to expectations, a tour with the Red Arrows can mean a pilot sees more of his family than he might do on a front line squadron.

Squadron Leader Al Chubb, who joined the Team in 1985 from a Phantom squadron in Germany, says, "It's much more relaxed here. The pace was horrendous in Germany. When my wife learnt that I was coming here, all her friends said, 'The Red Arrows – you'll never see him,' and she quite rightly answered with 'Well, I don't see him now!' In fact I have more time at home now than I ever did before. During the season we are away for maybe two or three nights at a time, but usually it's not much more than that. In Germany I would suddenly go away for three or four weeks and I didn't always know when I would be back. During the winter at Scampton, I go in to work at about nine and I'm back home by five."

The display season can, however, be very difficult for families. The Team are always away at weekends and over Bank Holidays, although they do usually have a couple of days off during the week.

"It is a difficult tour for wives with young children," says Heather Thomas. "They really get the thin end of the wedge. There are few perks as far as the wives are concerned. It is all right for people like me who don't have children. If the Team are away for a long trip like Indonesia, I can just decide to go off for a week or two. The girls with young children are stuck. They are tied by schools and during the summer holidays they are alone with the children all day and all night."

Heather met her husband when he was in the Red Arrows for the first time so she knew what she was letting herself in for. "I was delighted he was going back. I loved the first tour at Kemble, although it does mean that every wedding I've been to since he joined the Red Arrows, I've been to alone. People are beginning to think he is a figment of my imagination."

Some of the wives occasionally join their husbands at air shows but it doesn't always work. "You are a bit of a nuisance to them," says Anne Ploszek, the Team Manager's wife. "They have got a job to do and they are always so busy. It would be impossible if you had got children with you. I go occasionally, but I do feel as though I am tagging along. The organisers are very kind and accept you into the party but it is not quite the same as if they had said 'Do bring your wife along.' The receptions are part of the job."

Some wives are rather apprehensive about the dangers involved in flying with the Red Arrows, but Heather Thomas is not one of them. "I think it is safer than a front-line RAF job. It is so controlled and everything is so finely worked out that you do feel very safe about the whole thing. I am much more relaxed now than I was when Richard was flying Harriers. The Harrier is an amazing aircraft and he loved flying it but there does seem to be more risk and you do worry."

Most of the difficulties that wives experience come from being married to an RAF officer, rather than specifically to a Red Arrow. Servicemen in general will often be posted at quite short notice and they have little choice as to where they are going. It means suddenly moving house and changing schools and friends, and people who can't easily cope with that may find the Red Arrows posting and their husbands' constant absence in the summer even more difficult.

For women who want a career, being a Service wife is a very great disadvantage. "You are definitely segregated to the pile that people don't want to employ," says Anne Ploszek. "Teachers usually do quite well because they can do supply teaching but for most of us it is impossible. There is a lot of unemployment in Lincoln anyway and people don't want someone who will suddenly move away. But in this job the men do come home smiling. Most of the time they are so happy that, as long as you have your own interests, you are happy too."

While Richard Thomas was in Germany, the Red Arrows squadron was moved to RAF Scampton in Lincolnshire. At Kemble they had been almost an autonomous outfit, existing within the RAF but to some extent untouched by its rules and regulations. At RAF Scampton they were back in the fold. The station helps the Team with administration and discipline, and all operational aspects are dealt with direct by the Commandant of Central Flying School, which is also based there.

Warrant Officer George Thorne, now retired from the RAF but still living in Cirencester near RAF Kemble, was Team Adjutant there for eight years. The last five months of his service career, however, were spent commuting to Lincolnshire and he did not enjoy that at all. This was partly because of the travelling, but mostly because life was very different for the Red Arrows in Lincolnshire.

"I remember driving up to Scampton one Monday morning and picking up the phone to speak to the British Embassy in Washington to sort out a problem with our trip over to the States. The WRAF operator asked who was speaking and when I said who it was, she replied that only the Station Commander could make calls to Washington. Of course it was eventually sorted out but that was the kind of problem we faced. I think they slowly accepted us – whether they liked us is

another matter.

"Kemble is a lovely part of the country," says Brian Hoskins, "It is a bit more accessible than Scampton – although people still don't seem to have any trouble getting to the End-of-Season Guest Night, and I suspect they have just as many visitors in the winter.

"The main thing really is that Kemble was our airfield. There were other minor users but in the winter, as soon as the weather cleared, it was ours to go and practise. At Scampton there is Central Flying School and the whole station supervision. The station commander at Kemble was a Wing Commander Engineering Officer so the flying supervision stopped at OC (Officer Commanding) CFS Detachment, who was also a Wing Commander. Another advantage was that it was very close to our support airfield at RAF Lyneham, in

Wiltshire, and of course, everyone knew where we were. The Red Arrows had been at Kemble for years and that is where people expected to find us."

Despite the move from Kemble, as the end of his Harrier tour approached, Richard Thomas decided he would like to return to the Team as Leader. The Leader is the only member of the Team who is invited to come back for interview and is chosen without specific reference to the rest of the pilots. He is, however, always an ex-Team member and is therefore well known to them. It is important for him to be able to command the respect and loyalty of both the pilots and the ground crew and there is little doubt that Richard Thomas does just that. He appears easy-going with a pleasant, relaxed manner, but he expects a high standard from his squadron and he gets it. Although they say he rarely gets angry, he seems to

Above: Red Arrows Gnats flying over their home base of RAF Kemble in Gloucestershire

have total respect not only from those below him, but also from those above.

"The boss is the linchpin really," says Tony Lunnon-Wood. "He dictates the show, the way we live away on the road and the way the squadron runs. You have got to be a very special person to be Leader. The mental pressure on him is immense because it's totally unlike a normal squadron, where the boss can say, 'I've got a lot of paperwork coming in' or 'I've got some heavy decisions to make, pull me off the flying programme and I can pour all of my energy into that.' The boss can't do that here, he has to fly with us so not only is he doing all the niff-naff, he's also flying three, maybe four sorties a day. If the boss is ill, that's it, we don't fly. He is the most important person in every way.

"This would be a very, very difficult job to do if you didn't trust him. I've flown with two Leaders (Richard Thomas and John Blackwell, Leader from 1982–84), very different characters but both exceptional aviators, and they both have a way of sorting out the paperwork and still being able to put a lot of mental effort into the flying. I think that's the big difference between a good Leader and a bad Leader. The good ones don't take their problems into the air – or if they do, you never know about it. Once they close the canopy, they just think about the show and nothing else."

Squadron Leader Ted Ball, who was in the Red Arrows from 1983–85, agrees. "It's a very demanding job, far more demanding than I think is probably appreciated. It seems the easiest in some ways because he doesn't have to formate behind anybody, he just has to fly and everyone follows him, but it's actually by far the most difficult. He has to cope with all the problems of the terrain,

---

Above: Squadron Leader John Blackwell
straps in

locations, hazards and the wind and the weather. He's making instant decisions throughout the show, probably twenty or thirty decisions, and he's got to worry about eight guys behind him. When he gets airborne he probably also has a dozen other problems in his mind as well as how he's going to fly the show."

Ted Ball left the RAF in 1986 to live in Hong Kong and fly civil aircraft for Cathay Pacific. This is regarded among the pilots as probably the best civil flying job they can get – and Cathay Pacific now has quite a few ex-Red Arrows pilots on its books. Ted Ball regards his time in the Team as a very important stage in his life.

"I think it comes above your career. The RAF might dispute it, but it really is a bad career move although it is a fantastic flying job. It must be the best flying job that you could have anywhere in the world. It's just pure ocean-going fun and once you've mastered the skills, it's really only practice. There's nothing especially difficult about it, it's just endless practice, and it's thoroughly enjoyable. You meet so many people while you're on the Team, and they're nearly always such nice people. It was like a watershed for me because it really decided what I was going to do.

"Before I joined the Team I was quite keen to stay in the Air Force and make it my career, but I had my eyes opened during those three years. There is an awful lot going on in the world that you don't notice if you're just stuck in the Harrier Force. I don't think joining the Red Arrows makes people leave the Air Force, but people start to look at a wider range of things that they could do. You are a bit apart from the Air Force when you're on the road, meeting the public, but we all come from different backgrounds and wherever we went within the Air Force, someone would always know someone else really well. We did make an effort to join in with the other pilots. I think the image of the Red Arrows has improved over the years. The Team used to have a reputation as an elite, which put other people off, but the vast majority of people take us as we are. We're only another bunch of pilots doing a job."

Squadron Leader Tim Miller was in the Red Arrows from 1982–84, during the time their base moved from Kemble to Lincolnshire. He had wanted to join because he thought it would be a lot of fun, very demanding and very satisfying.

"I was proved absolutely right – it was definitely the best three years I've ever had. Mind you, my initial reaction to flying with the Team as a passenger was that, though it was very awe-inspiring, it was dangerous. I thought it was a supervisor's nightmare and shouldn't be allowed – but it was only because I was totally ignorant and hadn't yet seen the care and attention to detail that goes into the flying. Until you have flown with them as a pilot you don't actually understand how it all works."

From October 1987 Tim Miller is taking on an even more demanding job. He will be Richard Thomas's successor; the new Red Arrows Leader for the 1988 to 1990 seasons.

"You don't apply for the job. They look around and see who fits the criteria and then you are asked if you are interested. If you are, you and the other candidates are interviewed by a series of senior officers. The Leader has to be someone who has flown with the Team and who is now a Squadron Leader of about thirty-five or under. I am absolutely delighted to have been chosen although it would be naïve to think that it will be as much fun as being in the Team the first time. It will probably be more rewarding but I know it will be busier. I don't think Richard takes any time off at all. He has been a very popular Leader, it will be difficult to fill his boots. There are a lot of people in that kind of position of true leadership who are not very pleasant when they tell people what to do and how to do it. Richard is very good at that, he won't be easy to follow. I expect my style of leadership will be similar to his, though, because we are quite similar people. In any case, I intend to take a good summer holiday with the family before I go to Scampton. I certainly won't get one for the next three years."

Each year the Red Arrows usually perform over a hundred displays in Britain and abroad, and the careful planning and organisation that goes into the Team's schedule results in the vast majority of displays and trips away taking place without incident.

Occasionally, however, British summer weather takes a decisive hand and the weekend at Biggin Hill, which takes place early in the calendar, suffers regularly. In 1986 the Team had planned to arrive on the Saturday to display that afternoon. Unfortunately the persistent very low cloud base would not lift and the Team could not land. The wives back home at Scampton, who usually do at least know exactly where their husbands will be, suddenly found their planned supper party gate-crashed by unexpected guests.

The ground crew were operating that weekend without a Hercules. They had left Scampton early in the morning by road and had arrived safely at Biggin Hill as planned. The only problem was that they were now at one end of the country while the aircraft were at the other! Luckily the weather improved for the Sunday and the crowds were delighted to see the Red Arrows arrive. As they swept over the the runway in "Mange" formation (with the Manager flying the tenth aircraft) the air show really came alive. The skies stayed dull for most of the day but then halfway through the Arrows' display the clouds parted and the Team finished against a background of sparkling blue. It was a perfect end to an air show that had nearly been ruined.

★   ★   ★

Later in the season the Team were due to perform their 2,000th display at Hurn airport in Bournemouth. 1986 was also the 21st season of the Red Arrows and great celebrations were planned. Various British companies had been approached to see whether they would like to sponsor the show at which the Red Arrows' 2,000th display would be performed and there was some surprise that no-one came forward to do so. In the end it was sponsored by TV South and Renault UK.

Unfortunately the wet summer weather nearly ruined the celebrations. It prevented a proper show and the Team finally had to perform their shortest, lowest display ever – all they could do was taxi the aircraft across the runway to where Renault and the crowds awaited them! They were marshalled in by a selection of pretty girls in yellow jumpsuits and the head of Renault UK presented the Team Leader with an engraved granite slab as a memento of the occasion. All the pilots and ground crew were given large leather diaries and special non-alcoholic champagne was served. The French hosts quickly replaced it with the real stuff when the pilots returned, having taxied the jets back to their parking spaces.

After a quick drink, the Team were collected by the coach which was to be their transport for the weekend and taken to change out of their flying kit for the evening reception. Once dressed in their standard wear for civilian parties (grey slacks, blue blazers, striped shirts and Red Arrows ties), they posed for photographs in front of the coach, which had been lent to the show's organisers by a local firm. The driver was clearly enjoying himself: "It's like taking royalty round isn't it?" he said happily. The Team then made a flying visit to a company cocktail party and after several more photographs and one very hurried drink, they had to leave for the Renault reception.

Renault had organised a large party to celebrate the 21st birthday and 2,000th display, complete with a loud and enthusiastic band, speeches, a cabaret, a disco and a *Page Three* girl popping out of a birthday cake. There were pilots from other display teams, ex-Red Arrows members, local dignitaries and other distinguished guests.

Although the celebrations did not end until very late, the Team Leader, Richard Thomas, rose early to fit in his usual morning run. Also, whenever he can, he travels with a set of golf clubs.

Like Tim Miller, his successor, he is a golf fanatic and usually manages to find time to play a round – experience has taught him which airfields have nearby golf courses (the American Air Force bases sometimes have their own). It not only helps him keep fit but is good relaxation away from the aircraft and the pressures of his job.

Left: Squadron Leader Richard Thomas in the Briefing Room at RAF Scampton where manoeuvres are planned and displays discussed

Above: A hurried lunch taken at Hurn airport before the Team perform their 2,000th show. Soft drinks only of course!

Below: The End-of-Season Guest Night in 1986 was a very special evening. Over forty ex-Red Arrows made the journey up to Scampton to join other guests

On the Sunday morning the whole Team had to leave the hotel quite early to see Squadron Leader Thomas present flying scholarships, awarded by the International Air Tattoo, to a group of physically handicapped young men. (As sometimes happens under the direction of the Team Manager, the pilots found they had arrived with too much time to spare, time which they felt would have been better spent back at the hotel. One of them was heard to mutter that the Manager 'suffered from terminal organisation'.) When Richard Thomas eventually presented the scholarships, he had to give a speech, which he did, as usual, with deceptive ease – being Leader requires even more than exceptional flying skills and the ability to deal with people and cope with paperwork.

In the afternoon, the spectators were rewarded for their patience. The skies cleared enough for the Team to display and they prepared to take off. Just as they were about to taxi, Flight Lieutenant Collins suddenly noticed a caption (warning light) flicker on and so the aircraft could not fly. Leaving the ground crew to cope with the problem, he jumped out and ran to talk to the Team Leader. The spare aircraft was, unusually, not fitted with smoke and so Pete Collins took the Leader's jet to preserve the symmetry of the display.

Richard Thomas, showing the style practised on so many early morning runs, had to sprint the length of the line to get into the spare and lead the aircraft out to display on time. Despite the problems and the continued dull weather the display was very well received and delighted the crowd. The 2,000th show had at last officially taken place.

★   ★   ★

Whenever they are away for a few days, the pilots and ground crew are often required to attend receptions and parties, and they have to be careful. While the engineers always make sure they are on time and ready for work the next morning, they are still able to enjoy themselves and stay up fairly late. Alcohol and flying, however, simply do not mix.

"You never drink during the day when you have got a display to fly," says Tony Lunnon-Wood. "Even if the display is late in the afternoon – you just don't do it. There are two rules really. If you want to drink the day before a show, you really must leave the bar by nine or ten, or go on to water. Most days on the road you don't have to get up too early so you can still get plenty of sleep. You are always aware that if you do make a mistake you are letting down eight other blokes who are working very hard to do a good show. You learn your own limits very quickly and you make sure you get enough sleep to be right the next day. It's just self-discipline really."

In addition to the pilots' main jobs, they each have secondary duties to fulfil which range from those which traditionally go to the "new boys" and cover all aspects of publicity and answering mail, to the problems of arranging visits and lectures, ensuring the coffee bar in the Crew Room is well-stocked, dealing with customs officials and navigating the Team around the world.

The navigation is planned in the aptly named Nav/Planning Room while the "office" work is usually done in the Pilots' Quiet Room next door. All the air crew's rooms at the squadron lead off one long corridor on the first floor in a building which is mostly taken up with a huge hangar housing the aircraft. The ground floor is the engineers' territory.

The first floor has a small room known as the cinema at one end, where visitors can see films and slides about the Team, and the Briefing Room at the other. Framed photographs of displays and previous Red Arrow Teams line the walls opposite squadron plaques given to the Team – and opposite posters reminding the pilots to "Eject in Time". In the middle of this corridor is the reception area to which all visitors to the squadron are initially directed. Large glass cabinets protect many expensive gifts presented to the Red Arrows over the years, among which are silver salvers, cups, statuettes, a sword and a beautiful dagger presented to the Team by the King of Morocco. Another gift, a huge polished propeller, hangs on one wall – a bright idea from a host who wanted a special gift for the Team who has everything. On another wall, in their correct positions in the formation, are individual pictures of each of the current Team.

For anyone wanting one of the pilots in person, the best bet is probably the Crew Room. This is strategically placed between the Briefing Room and the Pilots' Quiet Room and is where they all congregate to make tea and coffee, eat biscuits and talk. An uninitiated visitor may not understand the continual banter that goes on over the coffee bar, but it is easy to see how well the pilots get on. They are all highly talented individuals with very different characters, but the method of selection and the nature of their work mean that they are, first and foremost, a team. They are doing a job they enjoy, working with people they respect and the jokes and banter are an integral part of the close relationships that are formed.

Exciting photographs of the Red Arrows adorn the walls of the Crew Room, alongside ones presented to them by other display teams. At the end of the room are the Team diaries. They are a detailed, chronological – though totally unofficial – record of all the Red Arrows Teams over the years. The diary is written up each year by one of the pilots, but although notable events, detachments in Cyprus, celebrations and long trips abroad all have their place, the diaries are essentially a private record. They are full of jokes and pictures that usually mean little to an outsider but which will always remind the pilots of their years with the Team.

One event in 1986 is unlikely to escape the diarist's notice, an event which proves that despite all the preparation and organisation that goes into the Red Arrows, sometimes totally unexpected things can happen.

They were based for the weekend at a foreign air base and were due to display at a nearby air show on the Monday. When the Red Arrows tried to leave for the display, a misunderstanding over an unfiled flight plan ended up with some of the Team with their hands up, looking down the barrel of a gun. It was a scene more reminiscent of the Wild West than the English countryside.

Incidents like that one are definitely exceptional, but all the pilots remember days during their three years when things did not go quite as planned.

Flight Lieutenant Pete Lees left the Team in 1986. He had become known as the master of the one-liner, and the other pilots delighted in his comment when a Sainsbury's plastic bag blew across the runway as they were all waiting to taxi. They watched it go, and after a pause they heard over the radio, "Good FOD costs less at Sainsburys," from Pete Lees. Foreign Object Damage is something the pilots try to avoid, but Pete Lees had to face a different problem during his first season with the Team in 1984.

"We were based at Exeter for the weekend in late August and doing a show in Sidmouth. It was basically a flat show because of the low cloud base but as we were coming to the end of the display the cloud was breaking up and so we pulled up to do a Vixen Break. I was No. 8 and on the outside of the loop and as we got to 90° nose up, I felt a slight vibration. I thought it was strange because you don't normally hit buffet until you are over the top and it is connected with how much you are pulling. I just had time to think, 'that's not right' when there was an incredibly loud bang and vibration and whirring. I immediately rolled away from the formation and told the boss on the radio that I thought I had had an engine surge. That is when the air flow to the engine is disturbed and you get too much fuel pumped in and not enough air. The mixture is all wrong and the engine vibrates and overheats.

"The standard drill is to shut the engine down and then start it up immediately, holding the relight button. I did this and the engine relit in surge. Even when the engine was closed down there was still a lot of vibration which indicated a mechanical failure so I thought I probably had more than a straightforward surge. I had another go at relight and by now I was down to about 3,000 feet.

"I told the boss that I thought I might have to eject because I couldn't get the engine started. The

Above: Flying down the runway at their home base, the Team practise
the manoeuvres that have made them world-famous

Right: Walking back from the aircraft, from left to right, Flight Lieutenant
Pete Lees, Squadron Leader Richard Thomas and Flight Lieutenant
Pete Collins discuss the practice. Squadron Leader Gordon Hannam is
in the background

airport from which we were operating was too far for me to glide and there was really no alternative. In the end it was probably one of the easiest decisions I've ever made. I was straight and level descending in a glide out over the sea. I had no compunction at all about pulling the handle. 'Eject in time!' (on posters back at Scampton) was very much in the forefront of my mind. I was quite high and had we been at an airfield I might have been able to do a forced landing and save the aeroplane. It is something we practise a lot.

"I suppose it was only about a minute from rolling away from the main formation to pulling the handle but it seemed an eternity. When I did eject it all happened very quickly. I can remember my legs being pulled in by the leg restraints and then my head was thrown down into my lap. I could see grey smoke, presumably the rocket exhaust, going away between my legs. As the seat goes up there is a force of about 20*g* but as it is a rocket rather than a great big bang, it is a relatively smooth acceleration.

"Below a certain height the connections to the seat are severed, the parachute pulls you out of it and the seat just falls away leaving the dinghy-pack attached to the harness. The next thing I knew I was dangling above the water. I realised I had cut my face a bit because I could feel some blood. It was grazed by tiny lead pellets from the Miniature Detonating Cord (MDC) on the canopy. You can still see the blue staining on my cheek. As soon as you pull the handle, the MDC fires and blows the canopy.

"I had a look at the aeroplane and saw it go in a lazy right hand turn out to sea, bounce once and then go down. That morning someone had tried to persuade me to have a swim and I had declined because I thought it was too cold. I remember thinking as I approached the sea, 'Oh well, I'll see how warm it is now.' It was actually quite pleasant and I just ran through the drill and got into the dinghy. I had already seen a launch coming towards me and within two minutes of being in the dinghy there was a boat alongside me.

"The Inshore Lifeboat picked me up and I was taken by helicopter to Exeter Hospital where I stayed overnight. They had a quick look at me and did a few X-rays. Fortunately I had done no damage at all, apart from cutting my cheek. The doctors weren't finished with me though. The next day I was transferred to RAF Wroughton for more X-rays and then the following day I went to RAF Halton for even more extensive X-rays. They pumped a bit of radioactive dye into me and then looked to see if I had any minute fractures. They also examined my eyes very carefully to see if I had any MDC damage in them and then on the Sunday I went back home.

"On the Monday morning I went flying with one of the other pilots just to get the feel of the aeroplane again. I felt fine but I'm very glad that I was back in the cockpit so quickly. Had I had any length of time off, I think I might have thought twice about it, but as it was it didn't bother me at all. We then did a practice and the next day we were off to Farnborough. It was a high pressure visit because we had to do an arrival display and the Prime Minister was there, but I got back in the groove again very quickly. I did think a bit as we came up to the Vixen Loop but that was all.

"I had total confidence in the ejection seat because Martin-Baker seats are renowned for being exceptionally good, and the only time they don't work is when they are used out of limits. I was well strapped in at a relatively low speed and I had no hesitation at all about pulling the handle. I think you might get more problems with a high speed ejection, and I am lucky in that I am the right sort of build to eject. It is best to be squat and stocky. If you are tall you might catch your knees on the way out or stretch your neck and crack a vertebra. You don't train on the seat but it was very straightforward and did everything for you. I think perhaps it gave everyone on the squadron extra confidence – it's nice to know that things work as they are supposed to."

Pete Lees' helmet, complete with pitting caused by the MDC detonating, now has pride of place along with other "trophies" in a glass cabinet at the Central Flying School at Scampton.

The RAF Board of Enquiry, which is always convened immediately an aircraft crashes, found that dissimilar metals in the low pressure compressor had caused fatigue cracks where the rotor blades joined the drum. After the enquiry, phosphor-bronze bushes were fitted in all Hawk engines at the critical point and this eliminated the problem.

By the end of 1986, the Red Arrows Teams had, over the years, clocked up over 46,000 flying hours and given 2,105 displays in thirty-four different countries, but despite the immense skill of the pilots and the reliability of their aircraft, there is still an element of risk in fast jet flying and close formation aerobatics. Seven pilots were killed flying in the Gnats, including one particularly tragic accident in 1971, when two new members of the Team flying as back seat passengers died along with the Synchro Pair when their aircraft touched. Another two pilots were killed together when a previous Team Leader visiting Kemble was also being given a ride.

Not surprisingly, it was incidents like these which led to the RAF drastically cutting back on the numbers of people allowed to fly with the team. Apart from prospective Team members and senior RAF officers directly responsible for the Red Arrows, very few people fly in practice displays, and those who do must fly with the Team Leader. Since the Hawks came to the Team, they have not had one fatality. Four Hawks have crashed either through mechanical failure or human error which, though rare, can never be totally eliminated, but luckily the pilots have all ejected safely.

For most pilots their most memorable days on the Team are concerned with far happier times. Some, like Squadron Leader Miller, remember displaying over Venice in the evening sun, and others, like Group Captain Dickie Duckett, find it difficult to forget their final display with the Team. If new Team members are vulnerable to being caught by jokers, a Team Leader nearing the end of his reign is even more so.

As a Flight Lieutenant, Dickie Duckett had first been in the Red Arrows from 1968–70. He returned as a Squadron Leader to lead the Team from 1975–76. Like many of his successors, he is a keen golfer, and his last display as Leader was to be over a golf course near the Severn Bridge during the Dunlop Masters Golf Tournament.

"As we came to the end of the display, we did our final bomb burst, splitting up to nine points of the compass. We were then supposed to turn to a particular heading and meet up at the Severn Bridge. I headed off to the agreed rendezvous – what I didn't know was that the other chaps had already planned to head off in another direction, join up and go straight back to Kemble. As I was flying to the Bridge, they were continuing to say the normal things over the radio as if they were coming in to join me and it was a few minutes before I realised that there wasn't actually anyone in sight.

"They got back to Kemble as fast as possible to land, get the champagne out and welcome me back from my last display. When I realised that they had done something a bit tricky, I tried to get them worried. I hung around for as long as I could before I went back – but I think they just drank more champagne! I think Brian Hoskins was probably the ring-leader, he was my deputy. He shouldn't have been surprised when a similar thing happened to him when he led the Team!"

Brian Hoskins was, in fact, caught out in almost exactly the same way. No Team Leader ever thinks his Team will desert him – especially when they decide to get their leaving present in before the end of the season:

"It has become traditional for the Team to leave a Leader at the end of a final display, or to try and get him to fly off in the wrong direction. You are sort of expecting it but of course when you get ready for a particular display, your mind is only on that and can easily be distracted. The display in Jersey takes place sometime in September and we had several to do after it so I was totally unprepared.

"The Team told me that we were supposed to be doing a fly-past over Alderney after the display and they produced maps for me to use. I spoke to

---

Page 138: One of the ground crew adjusts Flight Lieutenant Adrian Thurley's helmet. The Hercules transport aeroplane which accompanies the Team to distant displays becomes a travelling workshop – and gives the best view of the air show

Page 139: A four/five split looping and rolling. The display changes every year and, like this one, most manoeuvres come and go and then reappear in later years

the air-traffic controllers at Jersey and they said it was all right. There was nothing to make me believe it was anything but an organised fly-past.

"After the last manoeuvre, the Parasol Break or 'spaghetti', I was going to head off north to Alderney and they would join up with me in the normal way. Everything went according to plan. I set off, they made all the normal radio calls that I would expect and one aircraft even appeared in my mirror. If we have a transit to do after a display, I always make sure that I can see one or two join up. Everything appeared normal – and John Blackwell who was to be the next Leader was in the back seat. He was telling me about an aeroplane he could see between Alderney and the French coast which ensured that I kept my eyes looking forward to see it.

"After about five or six miles when I was beginning to feel slightly uneasy, though I didn't know why, I suddenly heard one of the pilots who was landing at Jersey come through on my radio. I asked if there was a problem because that is why he would have been landing, but no one answered. I suddenly realised what was going on – and sure enough, when I turned to fly back there was no-one in sight. The Team were on the ground at Jersey waiting with the champagne. They thought that I might be suspicious at the end of the season, so they made sure they caught me early."

The pilots often use old chestnuts against each other and, because the Team changes each year, they work again and again. If Spike Newbery had only known a little more about the unofficial history of the Team he might have heard of an incident at Kemble, when a new pilot waiting to take off from the runway had, by mistake, knocked his smoke button on. The sun was shining into the cockpit which prevented him seeing the warning light. One of the other pilots eventually told him on the radio – but when he returned to the Crew Room an "irate member of the public" rang to complain that his car had been damaged while parked in a lay-by outside the perimeter fence of the airfield . . .

As the end of the 1986 season approached, Pete Lees, Tony Lunnon-Wood and Squadron Leader Gordon Hannam, who had been the Deputy Leader that year, had to prepare to leave. Gordon Hannam had arrived on the Team very suddenly in March 1984 when one of the Synchro Pair had crashed in Cyprus at the start of the final two weeks' training. The pilot had had a miraculous escape and was unhurt but he had not been allowed to continue. He had miscalculated his height and was not able to complete the bottom cross of an Opposition Loop. As he tried to pull out from the dive, he almost succeeded, but the tail of the jet hit the runway and the aeroplane exploded in a cloud of thick black smoke.

"We all thought he was dead," said Tim Miller, who was in the Team at the time. "We re-grouped, landed and could see bits of red aeroplane everywhere. There was no sign of the pilot. Then the Squadron Leader Ops Henry Ploszek, the current Team Manager, who had gone out to the crash, turned and gave us the thumbs up! The pilot was okay, all he had were a few cuts and bruises. I saw him in hospital about twenty minutes later and he was fine. He must be the luckiest man alive – ever!"

Apparently the impact had fired the ejection seat, but the rocket motors which take the seat out of the aeroplane had been crushed. The drogue gun which normally fires once the seat is clear of the aircraft, and pulls out the main parachute, had fired through the canopy and the parachute pulled the pilot out of his seat, depositing him safely on the ground.

Gordan Hannam found himself with three days' notice to fly out and join the Team. "I had applied to the Arrows for the 1985 season but at that stage they hadn't even published the short list. I was told on Tuesday night that I had been picked to replace the pilot who had crashed and I had to be at Heathrow at 9.30 on the Saturday. It had all happened so quickly that Carole, my wife, knew nothing about it. I had to leave her to pack up the house and get the children into schools while I went off. I arrived in Cyprus on the Saturday and spent that evening in the bar. The next day I was writing the publicity material for the Team and on the

Monday morning they gave me a red suit. I had to stand there for the publicity photographs and I felt awful, I hadn't even flown yet!"

The Team were given an extra nine weeks in Cyprus to work up the display but they managed to do it in six. Because the Arrows were staying away for longer than usual, the candidates for the 1985 season were sent to have their interviews and to fly with the Team while they were in Cyprus. Squadron leader Hannam found himself discussing who should join the Team the following year, before he himself had ever flown a display with them.

Despite his unorthodox entry into the Red Arrows, his two and a half years with the Team passed smoothly and very enjoyably.

"What really stands out is how quickly the time has gone," he says. "It seems like only yesterday when I was sitting here waiting to see if I was going. The first year you are finding your feet, the second you get a bit more comfortable with the whole business, thinking you have ages to go and then suddenly it is your last year and suddenly it has gone!"

All the pilots find that the time goes too quickly but they also feel that three years is probably the right length of time for the job. Pete Lees spoke for them all when he said:

"I've had a fantastic time. I wouldn't have changed it for the world. I joined the Team because it was my idea of the best job in the Air Force, best flying, best way of life. I will certainly miss it, but we are all conditioned to three years and come two years and nine months you are beginning to look forward to new pastures."

The season does not officially end until the End-of-Season Guest Night which takes place at the beginning of October. Over a hundred people are invited to the dinner each year, and these range from ex-Team members to senior captains of industries with which the Team are associated, and people who have worked closely with them during the season. As is traditional with many Service dinners, it is basically a stag night. Wives are not invited – although the occasional female who has a connection with the Team in her own right may be lucky enough to receive an invitation.

The serving officers wear mess kit, the civilian guests dinner jackets and the tables are decorated with the squadron silver. The food is always delicious and the service is very formal. Too much talking and a half-eaten course will be whipped away with the other plates. The serving officers are used to this – an unwary guest learns fast.

The Guest Night at the end of the 1986 season was particularly memorable. As the season marked the 21st birthday of the Red Arrows, the pilots decided to persuade as many ex-Team members as possible to attend. Over forty of them made the journey up to Scampton, including seven out of the eight pilots from the original Team. Most of them had long gone their separate ways and were delighted to renew old friendships. It made the evening very special and many people did not get to bed until well into the early hours.

The third-year pilots do not actually leave the Red Arrows until the End-of-Season Guest Night each year and until then, the three new pilots are not part of the Team. It is a tradition that on the stroke of midnight after the dinner, the old pilots become ex-Red Arrows and the new ones take their places in the Team. There is always an element of sadness at this time. However much the pilots profess to be looking forward to their new jobs, they have spent the season living and working closely with eight other men and now they are moving on. The Synchro Pair have worked to become a particularly tight unit, developing an almost telepathic communication and a total trust in each other. Now the old Synchro 2 must take over and find that same level of communication in another pilot.

Suddenly the whole Team who have worked together to perfect the displays and delight the public are split up. The new Team have to start again from the beginning. The new pilots have to learn the display, the old pilots have to get used to new positions. Until the end of their winter training when they are once again cleared to fly in front of the public they practise in green flying suits – the Red Arrows as a performing team do not yet exist.

CHAPTER FIVE
THE GROUND CREW

Although the public only notice the nine pilots and the Team Manager giving the commentary at air shows, they are only the tip of the Red Arrows iceberg. Behind the Team there are about seventy-five ground crew whose duty it is to service the aeroplanes and make sure that there are always nine pristine Hawks ready to give a display. These men are a vital part of the Red Arrows squadron. The pilots are in the public eye and have the "glamorous" jobs, but they would literally never get off the ground without the technical back-up and dedication of the engineers.

The travelling ground crew, known usually as the "first-line", are the part of the squadron that the public do sometimes see. They are the men who travel with the Team to distant displays, either in the back seats of the jets or in a Hercules transport aeroplane. It is their job to service the aeroplanes on the road and to cope with any but the most serious problems that may occur.

In 1985 Flight Lieutenant John Chantry joined the Team as first-line Engineering Officer. He flies behind the Team Manager in the spare aircraft and the other nine aircraft carry ground crew in the back. These ground crew are known as the "Circus" (from "Flying Circus") and once the season starts they stay in the same aircraft with the same pilot and their name is painted on the aircraft under his.

The Circus are chosen each year from the first-line engineers. All the first-line must be medically fit to fly in the jets and they have the same medical examinations as the air crew. This means that any

Above: First-line wait to marshall their aircraft into line

Right: The Hercules has to carry over fourteen tons of men and equipment each time it goes away with the Team

one of them could, at short notice, take a back seat if it were necessary. The Circus leader and one or two others may stay for more than one season but the places are coveted and most of first-line want a seat in a Hawk. The general feeling is that a place in the Circus is probably the most varied and exciting ground crew job in the RAF.

Flying in the jets is part of the job and the Circus, along with the rest of first-line who go by Hercules or sometimes by road, spend the summer travelling round Britain and abroad. They go to places they have never been to before and meet people from all walks of life – and they meet them as the Red Arrows ground crew, an essential support for the famous aerobatic team. "The way I look at it," says one of the Circus, "is that there are only nine people in the whole of the Air Force doing this job – and I'm one of them."

There must always be a good cross-section of skills within the Circus, as they may find themselves coping alone when the rest of the ground crew are based elsewhere. It would be no good having a problem with an electrical system, if the Circus was made up entirely of air frame specialists. Although it is a popular job, however, not all first-line want to do it. "I've had the occasional flight, but I wouldn't want to do it all the time," says one; "It's not for the faint-hearted."

Flying behind the pilots is not always easy and at the beginning of the season when they start flying, most of the Circus will feel airsick. Even one of the Engineering Officers, who subsequently flew constantly during his two years with the Team, found his first flight difficult. Before he joined the squadron, he had been invited to go away with the Team for a weekend to see how they worked. He hadn't done any regular flying before, and when they flew back from Germany there was a lot of movement and he was ill – and he missed the sick bag! He did not make much mess and cleaned it up himself but, of course, the rest of the squadron, especially the ground crew, thought it was very funny.

Whenever the Team are due to fly, the back-seater does the pilot's pre-flight checks. On other squadrons, the pilot will always do his own walk round, but the Red Arrows are often so short of time, especially if they are performing three displays in one afternoon, that the ground crew do them. It means there has to be a good relationship and a lot of trust between them because the pilot is relying on his back-seater to do the checks properly.

The good relationship between pilots and ground crew extends beyond the cockpit to the whole of the engineering back-up, and is one of the ways in which the Red Arrows Squadron is quite unlike other RAF units. Most RAF pilots would know some of the handling flight (the first-line engineering section), but they would probably never come into contact with any of the rectification ground crew or second-line engineers. These are the men who service the aeroplanes and cope with any serious problems that may arise.

Most RAF stations have centralised servicing, which the squadrons would use for routine maintenance and the rectification of all but the most minor faults. The Red Arrows squadron has its own second-line engineers, and the vast majority of work done on the Hawks is done in the Red Arrows' hangar. The pilots quickly get to know both the first- and second-line ground crew – they know better than anyone how much they rely on the professional expertise of the engineers to keep their aircraft safely in the air. The Red Arrows are nothing if not a team.

During the display season, the Team have several different methods of travelling around the country. If they are displaying near home, they may take off from RAF Scampton, fly to the display site, display without landing and then return to their home base. In that case the first-line ground crew will have refuelled the aircraft, pumped the diesel/dye mix into the smoke pods and thoroughly checked the aircraft before the flight. They will then marshall the Team out onto the taxiway and away they go.

If the Red Arrows are going slightly further afield for a single display they do what is known as a "Circus Push". The ten ground crew (including the Engineering Officer) who travel behind the pilots will accompany them to an airfield near the display site. The aeroplanes will already be carrying the diesel and dye for the display, but they will land to unload the ground crew. The engineers then refuel the aircraft and do the turn-round checks necessary for the Team to take off again.

Each Circus member has a torch, a spanner, a screwdriver, keys and a padlock to secure the aircraft and a tin of Sparkle to clean the canopy. With this basic equipment they can do the turn-round checks, but if there were suddenly any real problems they would have to call up extra help from Scampton. The pilots then fly to the display site, display and return to refuel and pick up their ground crew for the flight back to Scampton. During the pre-season organisation, the Team Manager or his staff will have contacted the airfield and requested permission for the Red Arrows to land. They will also have asked them to provide fuel, catering facilities and anything else that might be needed.

If the Team is displaying far from Scampton or doing several displays away from base, they have to take a great deal more equipment and many more ground crew. The preferred method and the one which, in the past, was more usual, is for the Team to be accompanied by a Hercules transport aeroplane. This can carry a large amount of equipment and anything up to about twenty ground crew.

These men who, along with the Circus, make up first-line engineering, are expected to be able to cope with any of the more usual problems that might arise with the aircraft while they are on the road. The Hercules, though propeller driven, is regarded as the eleventh jet, and just like the Hawks it must arrive at the destination on time. Its loading is a precise and well-rehearsed operation to ensure that the weights are properly balanced and that the most frequently needed equipment is most accessible. A team from first-line are responsible for loading the Hercules and they pack everything in like a three-dimensional jigsaw.

On average the Hercules has to carry about fourteen and a half tons of men and equipment, including any spares that might be needed for the aircraft, tools, a jack trolley, hydraulic rigs, spare flying suits and helmets, the dye rig, barrels of dye, a metro van, a Land-rover, documentation box and all the baggage that accompanies thirty ground crew, the Engineering Officer, the Manager and nine pilots – including the Team Leader's golf clubs. The only thing that appears to be forgotten is that twenty engineers also have to fit in. They are squeezed along the sides of the aircraft with their backs to the fuselage and their legs tucked in beside piles of equipment. The most comfortable seats, the roof of the Land-rover and a couple of hammocks, are quickly occupied and the men settle down for the flight, equipped with indispensable earplugs (the Hercules is not a quiet machine), books and personal stereos. There is not a great deal of conversation – hardly possible in the circumstances – and many of the crew take the opportunity to sleep. They know well that as soon as they land they will be busy. If there are any problems with the aircraft or anything serious found during the After Flight inspection (or "AF" as it is called) they may have to work through the night to put it right.

In these days of cost-cutting, the RAF will not always have a Hercules available for the Team. They have to put in a bid for air frame hours like every other unit in the Air Force, and they do not have a particularly high priority. If they are not allocated a Hercules, the engineers load all their equipment onto an articulated lorry. One of them has to drive this, the "Queen Mary", to wherever the Red Arrows are to be based, and a bus transports all the ground crew.

Road support obviously takes much longer than flying in by Hercules and breakdowns, weather and traffic conditions can make life difficult. It is very important for the engineers and their equipment to arrive at a display site on time – and if an air show's traffic is proving too heavy, the ground crew have been known to get a police motor-bike escort through the crowds.

Road support works well when the Team are based firmly in one place, like Farnborough. If all

Left: On the flight-deck of the Hercules en route to the annual visit to
USAF Ramstein in West Germany

Above: The member of the ground crew in charge of loading the
Hercules seems to forget he has to fit in up to twenty men in addition to
all the equipment!

the displays take place over the airfield, or if the Team go to other sites only to display but not to land, the engineers will always be where they are needed. The difficulties arise if the aeroplanes land away from base, have a problem and all the spares are miles away. The Hercules acts as a travelling workshop. If it follows the Hawks around, the ground crew will have all the equipment and expertise necessary to deal with virtually any problem that is likely to occur. During the Falklands War in 1982, all available transport aircraft were too busy flying to and from Ascension Island to be called into service for the Team, and when they travelled to Germany the engineers had to take road support across the channel – and they still managed to arrive on time. Usually, however, the Team will always travel with a Hercules when they go abroad. The complications of taking so many men and so much equipment by road are too great to contemplate, except in very unusual circumstances.

After every flight, whether from Scampton or when they are away, each member of the Circus will carry out a thorough After Flight inspection of his aircraft. He checks the cockpit, both ejection seats and the instruments, cleans the canopy and the gauges and looks for wear on tyres, wear on brake units, systems leaks, cracks and anything else that might not be quite perfect. By the end of the day there will usually be something to do to every aeroplane before it is completely serviceable again. The first-line crew will deal with any routine problems. At Scampton anything more serious will usually be dealt with by the second-line engineers. The night-shift comes in at four o'clock, and they will work as long as necessary to ensure that the aircraft are all fully operational by the next morning.

Before any aircraft is flown the next day, the first-line engineer – again whether at Scampton or on the road – will do the Before Flight inspection, known as the "BF". He concentrates on the things that could leak during the night, like gas and tyre pressures and accumulators. The turn-round, which takes place between flights, is effectively a combination of an AF and a BF. The ground-crew member will put fuel in, and if the aeroplane is

about to be flown on display, he will solo it. This entails securing all the straps in the rear seat and covering it with an "apron" to ensure that nothing can flap about. He will also check the fatigue meter, reset switches in the cockpit, do an external check to make sure that there are no cracks or leaks and clean the canopy.

At high level the Hawks are very economical aircraft. Cruising at 36,000 feet, they will do five miles to the gallon – not much for the family saloon, but extremely good for an aeroplane which is covering seven miles every minute. When the Red Arrows flew out to Jakarta to display at the Far East Air Show in 1986, it was the Hawks' most ambitious trip yet. The Team travelled out with two Hercules, and the ground crew had to be prepared to cope with any problems that might arise during each Hawk's estimated sixty flying hours away from base. They even took a replacement engine in case they had major problems, and extra ground crew from the second-line engineering section. No-one was sorry when they returned home six weeks and 18,900 miles later with the engine still safely in its cradle.

Flight Lieutenant Chantry was very pleased with the performance of both the ground crew and the aircraft. "We took a lot of extra people so that if we had had a major problem we could have left a team of engineers behind to sort it out. The Circus worked particularly hard because there were several places where the Hawks would land to refuel but the Hercules would simply fly on to the next stop. I did once have to call in one of the Hercules when three tyres deflated after we landed on a particularly hot airfield. We had one spare with the jets but not three. I expected to have trouble with tyres because of heat and poor surfaces so the 'Hercs' carried about thirty spares between them and in the end we had used most of them. But out of 550 starts we only had problems with three aircraft. These were due mainly to dust and moisture getting into the electronic boxes. We just changed the boxes and the problems were solved.

"In the beginning we did have a few people keeling over in the heat. One chap in India had been working outside in the sun and he collapsed in the back of the Hercules. He had a total salt imbalance and had to go to the medical centre, but he recovered quite quickly. It was a lesson to everyone else. The other problem was tummy bugs. I think everyone suffered from that at some stage."

That particular problem must have been very unpleasant. Facilities in the Hercules are, to say the least, primitive, and it cannot have been easy on long flights to cope with upset stomachs on a crowded aeroplane.

"When we got home the aeroplanes were looking a bit shabby," says John Chantry. "All the leading edges needed cleaning and polishing because they had been in ideal conditions for corrosion, with dust and constant changes from dry to damp conditions and back. They all had to be thoroughly checked, and it was found that some of the fastening screws on the panels inside the cockpit were beginning to corrode. It wouldn't happen during a normal season but we had to change them and generally clean up the whole aircraft."

Every year, during the winter, three or four aircraft are sent away to RAF Brawdy in Wales to be repainted. This total respray takes about three weeks but, in addition, the aircraft will also need continual touching up throughout the year by station personnel from RAF Scampton. A heavy rainstorm during a transit flight can make quite a mess of the paintwork.

Occasionally, in any season, the Hawks may have minor problems while they are away which cannot be rectified on the spot. Flight Lieutenant Chantry will consult with the technicians and decide whether he can clear the aircraft to fly either until the end of the day, until the aircraft gets back to Scampton, or until the next scheduled servicing.

These "acceptable defects" are written into the aircraft's documents on a special page and might be anything from part of the navigation kit that had failed (which would not be a great problem for a Red Arrows jet flying in formation), to a minor dent caused by a bird strike, or a possible loose article in the cockpit.

Whether or not the aircraft can fly with a loose article depends very much on the nature of the article and where it has been lost. The engineers will try and locate it and they may even ask the pilot to take the aeroplane up and fly upside down to see if it drops onto the canopy. If at all possible, they want to avoid the final solution, removing the ejection seat. This is a big job and takes a long time. To minimise the danger of leaving things in the cockpit, the ground crew are not allowed to take any loose articles into the aircraft – anyone losing something in an aeroplane is not popular! For the same reason the use of tools on the aircraft is rigidly controlled. At Scampton all tools and small spare parts are kept in a storeroom adjacent to the hangar. The tools are hung on shadow boards and no one can remove one without leaving a tag in its place. These tags show not only who has it but on which aircraft he is working.

It is easy to see at a glance which tool is missing – and if there is no tag on the shadow, there is obviously a problem. When first-line go away with the Team, all the tools they take are booked out and then accounted for on the road in just the same way. A lost spanner would cause delay or, if left unnoticed in an aircraft engine, could easily cause an accident.

When the pilots are practising at Scampton during the winter, they will come downstairs from the Briefing Room and go along to First-Line Control. On the way they pass the Flying Clothing room, another responsibility of the first-line ground crew. Flying suits, g-suits, immersion suits (used for some exercises over water), helmets and all the special socks and underwear needed by the pilots are kept here. In addition, an ejection seat sits in the middle of the room. This is, of course, a very important piece of equipment. Once the pilot pulls the handle everything happens automatically and in less than three seconds he finds himself dangling safely in his parachute. Anyone flying with the Team will sit in the ejection seat in the Flying Clothing Room and be carefully briefed on what to do in an emergency. He will have to learn how to remove the "pins" (two keys which are the safety cut-out for the seat rocket and the canopy MDC)

Above: Pumping the diesel/dye mix into the aircraft is always the messiest and least favourite job but, **Right:** the brightly coloured smoke has become synonymous with the Red Arrows

before the flight, and to replace them when the aircraft has landed.

The ground crew member who helps a visitor strap into the aircraft, will check that the pins have been removed and the seat armed, but as the canopy must be closed first, the passenger will have to take them out himself.

He will be warned not to drop them but to put them into the stowage on the canopy rail. He will also be reminded not to cling on to the handle during violent manoeuvres. To reinforce the briefing, safety warnings and the ubiquitous "Eject in Time" are written up on posters on the walls. If this advice is taken, the Martin–Baker seat works both literally and metaphorically like clockwork.

The flying helmets have to be carefully fitted for each man and once this is done for the pilots and the Circus, their helmets are kept on a special rack in First-Line Control. When the pilots go through that room they must sign for their aeroplanes, before collecting their helmets and "walking". On their return they will sign the aircraft back in. This is a simple procedure at Scampton but less so when they are on the road. One of the first-line will be in charge of all the documentation for the Hawks and he must ensure that he gets signatures before and after each flight. He will usually catch them before the display when they are briefing at the wing – afterwards it can be more difficult. The pilots like to get away very quickly, so he is usually waiting for them as they land.

During the 1986 tour when the aircraft were away from Scampton for six weeks, Flight Lieutenant Lovejoy, who has commanded second-line engineering since 1984, went out to Indonesia with the first-line Engineering Officer and the ground crew. Usually, however, he remains at Scampton while Flight Lieutenant Chantry travels with the Team.

"I am called Team Engineer," says John Chantry. "On the road people often assume I do it all, just working with the Circus. My picture is in the main part of the brochure alongside the pilots and the Manager, and some people even think that I dash around looking after all the aeroplanes entirely

alone. They certainly don't realise that we have so much back-up at Scampton."

Flight Lieutenant Lovejoy has overall responsibility for making sure that the aeroplanes leave Scampton fully serviceable, and from 1st October every year the thorough winter servicing of each aircraft begins. This is the busiest period for the second-line engineers, and some of the first-line, who have less to do during the winter than during the display season, will help them. During this servicing (the "deep-winter strip"), three aircraft at a time are removed from the fleet and taken apart. They are completely refurbished, put back together, air tested and then returned to the flight line. It takes about three weeks to do each one and the engineers have to work particularly hard because the Team are busy training the three new pilots. Extra aircraft are brought in from RAF Valley to help spread the load but that also means that the ground crew have to cope with more aircraft than usual, in addition to having a hangar full of aircraft being serviced. These borrowed aircraft, know as "Raspberry Ripples" because of their red and white paint scheme, can easily be spotted in the sky over Lincolnshire during the winter, flying in formation with the Red Arrows' Hawks.

As each winter service is finished the aircraft are air tested. During the air tests Flight Lieutenant Lovejoy usually sits in the back seat behind one of the pilots.

"First of all we work our way up to 44,000 feet and on the way we check radios, navigation aids and all the systems. When we get to 44,000 feet, we start checking the aeroplane's handling behaviour, things like stalling her gently to see how she behaves. We work through the flight-test schedule, writing down all the instrument readings and noting engine performance.

"Once all those checks are done, then we start. A spin to the left, another to the right and she must recover from each within one and a half turns. The Hawk is, in fact, so reluctant to spin that you have to work very hard to get her to do so. When we've finished the spins, we come down at nearly the speed of sound, checking that the aeroplane handles properly and we then do the high speed run. She must do between 540 and 550 knots at 2,000 feet and be properly trimmed. It's almost hands and feet off – she must fly perfectly straight all by herself. At the end of all this we pull 5½g, and then we pull to 7½g – and that hurts. If she comes out of that without any buffet, porpoising or any unusual flight characteristics, she's deemed to be okay – and then we usually finish off with a loop to check her speed over the top. A full air test will take about an hour and a quarter. An engine air test which doesn't include the handling aspects takes about three-quarters of an hour."

Once the season has started, the pilots tend to keep the same aircraft, but the different demands made on the Hawks can cause problems. Although the Team spend most of their time flying together, the aeroplanes all consume different amounts of fatigue according to their positions in the formation. The wings are bent more or less, the fuselage is bent more or less and the aircraft is thrown around more or less. The aircraft have fatigue meters fitted, and each time the throttle opens and closes the clicker on the meter records one cycle.

"During the season we might change one or two over because of management of fatigue on the aircraft," says Flight Lieutenant Chantry. "But a lot of people are surprised to learn that the aircraft which do the weapons training pull a lot more g than we do. A lot of our manoeuvres are reasonably gentle although the Vixen Break is probably quite severe and the Synchro Pair give their aircraft a bit of a hammering in terms of fatigue."

Because the aeroplanes that fly in the Synchro Pair consume far greater levels of fatigue than the others, every ten displays the engineers will carry out NDT (Non-Destructive Testing) checks on them to search for cracks. They pass an electric current through the air frame and pick it up on an oscilloscope. If the current jumps a gap, it will show up as a blip and they will know that there is a crack and where it is.

Managing the Red Arrows' aircraft is a constant balancing act. The amount of fatigue consumed by the aircraft must be shared across the fleet and this means that every year they will fly in a different position in the formation. The Leader's aircraft, which would have a fairly easy, smooth ride one season, might well be in the Synchro slot the next.

Flight Lieutenant Lovejoy's major worry, thoughout the year and especially during the display season, is always fatigue – the aircraft's, not the pilots'! He is responsible for finding the right aircraft to fit the right slot each year and it isn't always easy.

"We try to share out the work load between the aeroplanes. We switch them all through the winter and we'll only come down hard on the season's aircraft generally the week before Cyprus, when we put the names on them. They stay the same for that season and then in the following winter I get all sorts of bribes from pilots wanting to remain in the same aircraft! The aircraft *are* very different. There is one which no-one wants. They claim she's a bit slow but during the air test she was found to be fine. There's obviously some slight problem so she is under review now and British Aerospace are going to come and have a look. We've done an awful lot of work on her but we can't find what's causing it.

"The ones that fly Nos 8 and 9 have really got to motor. They are the last ones tucking into the diamond over the top with Nos 6 and 7 slotting in between them. Nos 6, 7, 8 and 9 have all got to be speedy aeroplanes. We tried three aeroplanes in the No. 9 slot before settling on one, and the pilots don't like changing.

"The aeroplanes are slightly different in weight, slightly different in performance and handling and although they are all marvellous on their own, when you get them together as we do you really notice those differences."

In common with every other operational squadron in the RAF, the Red Arrows must keep meticulous and detailed records about their aircraft, and every Hawk has a long list of components which each have their own case history. The parts of the engine that rotate, like turbine discs and compressors, are the parts which

Left: At RAF Scampton each aircraft is completely stripped down and then refurbished during the winter servicing

Above: Flight Lieutenant Charlie McIlroy watches as Squadron Leader Richard Thomas discusses an aircraft's form 700, the servicing record, with Flight Lieutenant John Chantry, the Team Engineer and Chief Technician Fisher in First-Line Control

always cause the most worry. They are the parts which are under continual stress and are the most likely to come apart in the air. They all have set lives (calculated in terms of flying hours), and they are constantly monitored in terms of fatigue. When they get to a specific age, the engineers will replace them and thus prevent any possible problems.

Other parts are not subject to any form of stress but will deteriorate with age and must be replaced regularly. The explosives in the ejection seat are a good example of this. Every two years all the cartridges in the seat must be changed to ensure that they are always in perfect condition if needed.

To disrupt the flying as little as possible, the Engineering Officers will try to time as much work as they can for the scheduled servicings, but there might be something which must be checked every ten flying hours.

"The pilots sign the aircraft out before each sortie and then give them back when they return," says Frank Lovejoy. "We only loan them the aeroplanes. They have to fill in a 725 – a fatigue data sheet – after every flight. It shows what they've done and how they've done it. It records fuel loads, which of course affects the aircraft weight, number of occupants, stores carried on the wing, the pod which carries 250kg of liquid for the coloured smoke and which is all gone by the time they land, number of landings and so on. It all adds up to a picture of how the aeroplane has been used and how long it was used for. We also take the fatigue meter reading. The statistician gets all these numbers and works out the amounts of fatigue the aeroplane has used."

The engineers have huge filing systems to keep track of the paperwork and all the modifications have to be detailed. There is a very large number of them although only two are specifically for Red Arrows' Hawks. One is the smoke pod that goes underneath the aircraft and makes it possible to get the red, white and blue smoke, and the other is in the engine. It is the same engine that is in every Hawk but has a modified fuel control unit. It is like taking the governor out of a car so it accelerates faster, and although it has the same power as any

Hawk engine, it means that it can produce that power faster. As it is a fairly complicated modification it is done at the manufacturers.

Because of the modified engine in the Team's aircraft, the RAF Valley Hawks which are lent during the winter are only allowed to fly in certain positions in the formation. The Red Arrows' Standard Operating Procedure states that they must fly in positions 1, 2 or 3 – the gentlest slots which require the least power changes and acceleration.

Another recent modification undergone by all RAF Hawks, including those flown by the Red Arrows, is their conversion to a war role. They are now able to carry Sidewinder air-to-air missiles and a central gun pod, and in times of war they would be camouflaged for UK air-defence duties.

Just like civil aircraft, the Hawks each carry the equivalent of the Black Box flight recorder, known here as an ADR (Air Data Recorder). Every five flying hours the information recorded is extracted by computer in the GRAS room (Ground Replay Analysis System).

"We put the cassettes in and the machines will milk the disc to get the information," says Frank Lovejoy. "We then have a blank disc which can be replaced in the aeroplane. If there is an engine problem or one of the pilots says that a caption (a warning light on his systems board) has come on, we'll take the ADR out when he lands, milk it and produce a hard copy print-out and see what the problem is. It's like a spy in the cab."

Another very useful source of information about the aircraft engines, and one which allows the engineers to anticipate possible problems, is the early failure detection cell. Each engine has a series of magnetic plugs which attract any steel particles present from the oil as it passes. By examining these tiny particles the engineers can tell if bearings are breaking up. They plot growth rates of this debris on a chart and can see if there is a problem. In a new engine they expect to see a lot of dirt and dust because, like a car, it is running-in, but then this will level out. If it then starts to rise again, the engine is clearly beginning to wear. The engineers

Left: Refuelling the aircraft for the next flight. One of the ground crew is monitoring the fuel gauge in the cockpit

Overleaf: The ground crew tow a Hawk back into the hangar at the end of another day

can detect an increase in wear rates at Scampton and they will then send a sample to the Rolls Royce metallurgy department which will be able to pinpoint exactly which bearing is causing the problem.

Most squadrons in the RAF would expect to have seventy per cent serviceable aircraft every day; the Red Arrows need virtually a hundred per cent and during the display season the engineers must supply the Team with ten out of eleven aircraft every day. They are greatly helped, however, by the fact that the British Aerospace Hawk, compared with a front-line jet, is a fairly simple aeroplane. When the Red Arrows first took delivery of the Hawks, the engineers quickly realised that it was also far easier to maintain than its predecessor, the Gnat. Ground crew who worked on the Gnat do seem to have a soft spot for it and many people preferred its swept wing shape in the display, but there is no doubt that, by the time the Team received their new aeroplanes, the Gnat was feeling its age.

One of the engineers remembers it well: "In the last year of the Gnat, we seemed to leave an aeroplane behind at most of the places we displayed. They were getting so old and spares were very difficult to get. It wasn't a very good advertisement for the Air Force."

Over and above all the careful maintenance carried out throughout the year at Scampton, each Red Arrows Hawk is sent away to RAF Abingdon every five or six years. Here it will be given a "major" service, a complete and thorough overhaul which takes about eleven weeks and which goes into even greater detail than the annual deep-winter strip. At the end of this time it will be returned to the Team virtually "as new".

Apart from working on the routine servicing and the more complicated problems that occur at home, a team of second-line engineers may also be called out to wherever the Red Arrows are operating. If an aircraft has a serious problem which can't be dealt with by the first-line ground crew on the spot in the time available, the Team Engineer will call Flight Lieutenant Lovejoy who will send a specialist team from Scampton. In 1985 when the Red Arrows were on their way back from Cyprus, one of the aeroplanes had a brake malfunction, which resulted in both tyres bursting as they landed at a French airfield.

"It wasn't a normal skid," says Frank Lovejoy, "one wheel was locked solid and the aeroplane left the runway. It went onto rough scrubland and the pilot just managed to steer between some concrete blocks and bring it to rest.

"It happened on a Thursday morning. We spent the afternoon at Scampton getting ready and, because we didn't have a spare undercarriage, we had to take one off another aeroplane which took a bit of time. The braking system on the Hawk is electronically operated, so it spreads across several different trade areas and I had to take electricians, air frame people and engine people in case the aircraft had picked up other damage when it went off the runway.

"The seven of us left Scampton at midnight by truck, went down to Lyneham and loaded up the Hercules. It was on its way to Gibraltar but had been held at Lyneham to wait for us. We left at seven o'clock and got to France just before midday local time.

"We worked on the aeroplane from Friday lunchtime straight through until it was ready. We had to use torches at night – the French couldn't provide us with lights on the airfield. It was flown back by a pilot from Central Flying School on Monday lunchtime, and then we were stuck for nine days!"

It is extremely important for the first- and second-line ground crew to work well together and feel they are part of the same team. Although they have very different duties there is usually no problem, although there is always some rivalry between the two sides. It could look as if first-line have an easy time, stepping into the fully serviceable aircraft that second-line have provided, to fly off all over the world. But although they may seem to have the glamorous jobs when they travel with the Team, they do many mundane jobs both on the road and at Scampton which can be very repetitive.

The dirtiest part of the hangar – and the hardest to clean – is the "pod prep area", where the smoke pods are stripped down in the winter and the floor gets soaked with dye and diesel. The pods which fit underneath the aircraft are extremely heavy. They hold fifty gallons of diesel in the centre tank, ten gallons of diesel/dye mix in the front tank and ten gallons of diesel/dye mix in the back tank. Air pressure from the engine drives the mixture through three separate pipes to the exhaust at the back of the jet. The diesel produces the white smoke, and the dyes, mixed with it, give the red and blue smoke.

The pilots select the appropriate colour by using one of the three buttons on the top of the control column. The efficiency of the Hawk's engine has caused some problems for the Red Arrows. When they flew the Hawker Siddeley Gnat the high exhaust temperature, mixed with the diesel and dye, produced a deep-coloured smoke. The Rolls-Royce Adour engine which powers the Hawk is much more efficient and produces cooler exhaust – and that makes the colours less vivid.

The men from first-line who make up the dye team (the messiest and least favourite job) sometimes seem to spend all day in the British summer, in pouring rain, getting covered with blue and red dye as they pump it into the aeroplanes. They are often highly qualified tradesmen but because there is not that much trade work to be done, the travelling ground crew have to be adaptable, work closely as a team and help with whatever needs doing. Throughout the season when the Red Arrows are on the road, first-line do work hard, at odd hours and often in very difficult conditions, but of course their busiest time is usually when they are away from Scampton – and unseen by the second-line engineers.

"We don't get any choice who we have in the squadron," says Frank Lovejoy. "They may have had Hawk experience but we often get people coming straight from training. I think it says something for the Service that we rarely have any problems with the men we get. They all go on to second-line when they join us, which means I tend to have a mixture of the very young ones who are learning how we work and also the older, more senior tradesmen who work on the deep-winter strip.

"Sometimes we have men who go on to first-line and after one or two seasons they'll volunteer to come off, because they don't get a great deal of trade work. They'll decide to come back into second-line or go to other stations and get more experience of their proper trade. They'll be replaced by someone coming from second-line who has been taught how to do the jobs in the way we do it – and he's also got to get used to the way the Reds operate, no bank-holidays off, working every weekend during the summer, that sort of thing."

For all the ground crew, being part of the Red Arrows squadron is very different from other jobs in the Air Force. There are times when even the second-line don't know what is going to happen next. They work mostly in shifts so they can usually plan ahead, but sometimes they are called back in – and they may only have been home six or seven hours. The secret seems to be the team spirit which many people feel is much stronger than on other RAF squadrons. In the old days all squadrons were organised like the Red Arrows, but rising costs and defence cuts have forced economies. All squadrons have first-line ground crew, but the second-line would probably not be in the same hangar and might never see a pilot. All they see is the handling flight delivering a broken aeroplane, saying "Sorry chum, we've got a problem."

Whenever the Team display, one way or another the ground crew are there in the background. The second-line back at Scampton have provided ten fully serviceable aircraft for the pilots to fly and the first-line on the road refuel the jets, replace the diesel and dye, check and re-check the equipment, rectify any problems and put the covers on the aircraft at the end of the day. The travelling ground crew wear special blue flying suits, and as they watch the Team perform they are justly proud of their work. They know that without the support and expertise of the engineers, the Red Arrows would not be there.

CHAPTER SIX
PUBLIC RELATIONS

From the beginning of October each year the Red Arrows' hangar at RAF Scampton becomes a hive of activity. During the display season there are many days when all the aircraft, pilots and first-line ground crew are away at air shows and their home base is very quiet. Once the season is over, however, the second-line engineers come into their own. The hangar is filled with aeroplanes having their major services in addition to the ones the pilots are using for winter training. This is also the start of the constant stream of visitors who come to Scampton to see how the Team work.

During the display season, the pilots have very little time to talk at length to people and so they try to make up for it in the winter. Schools, busi-nessmen, Women's Institutes, associations and clubs of every kind either want to visit Scampton or ask for one of the Team to visit them and talk about the Red Arrows. Those who come to Scampton are shown around the hangar. They get an opportunity to see the beautiful gifts that have been presented to the Team over the years, and are given stickers and brochures which tell them about the squadron. They will look at the aeroplanes, meet those Team members who are there, watch anyone who is practising and listen to a talk with slides about the history of the Team and how it all works. To satisfy these customers, the sergeant who runs the motor transport (MT) section for the squadron and whose main responsibility lies in organising the fleet of cars, vans, refuellers, trucks and buses, also runs the Red Arrows shop. He sells T-shirts,

Above: Squadron Leader Richard Thomas presenting a flying scholarship awarded by the International Air Tattoo in memory of Sir Douglas Bader to one of a group of disabled young people

Right: Part of a specially mounted sortie for the Telegraph Sunday Magazine allowing the Team to reach a wider audience than the air show enthusiasts

models, badges and all kinds of souvenirs for the Team, and the money goes to the Red Arrows Trust.

The Trust is a charitable organisation set up to administer money raised by the sale of souvenirs and donations the Team receive for charity. Some of the donations are given to them after winter lectures. The pilots receive many requests for them to go and talk to interested groups during the training season and although these talks are free, the audience often ask to make a donation as a thank-you to the pilot. Any money he is given will either go straight to a specific charity or into the Red Arrows Trust, and each season the trustees decide who will benefit from it. Some of the money will go to the RAF Benevolent Fund, but the Team also like to support local charities and hospitals. Many of the donations are sent to STRUT (Short Term Residential Unit Trust) – a local short-stay home for handicapped children whose families need a few days away from the problems of coping at home. In addition to donating money from the Trust, the pilots also visit the home and other charities in the area.

Although they have a full winter training schedule, the pilots do manage to give about seventy lectures between them. The Team Leader is not usually involved, as both he and the Team Manager are always as busy in the winter as they are in the summer.

"We do get masses of people asking us to give lectures," says Squadron Leader Thomas. "It can get out of hand if people just think it's cheap entertainment, but we do try to do as many as possible. I am sometimes invited to be guest speaker at a dinner which is more work than giving a talk. I'm not showing slides, of course, and I can't go on about the Red Arrows the whole time, so it is different. I do also give the occasional lecture, but generally during the winter I'm first in in the morning and last out at night, so the guys are happy to leave me out of it."

When they join the Red Arrows, the pilots quickly realise that giving lectures is an important part of their job. "People on the Team are very

realistic," says Charlie McIlroy. "They know when they join that there will be a lot of hard work on the PR side and so they accept it. It is after all a public relations job. I don't mind giving lectures as long as there is a decent audience. Usually people are so enthusiastic about what you are doing that you get a very good reception."

Tony Lunnon-Wood agrees: "I can get great satisfaction out of giving lectures although a lot depends on where you are. You have a captive audience and they wouldn't be there unless they wanted to hear you. The only time you are disappointed is if you have driven three hours after flying maybe four trips, and when you arrive there are only a dozen people there. Then you have got another three hour drive back and you wonder if it's worth it. But it is all part of the job and it's great to get out and meet civilians and get some of the old propaganda across to them. They suddenly realise that we are here to do a job – not just the Red Arrows, but the Royal Air Force. Sometimes we are a nuisance but we don't do it deliberately – we are just trying to achieve an aim, and we have also got wives and families who hate noise. We can convert a lot of people and help them understand what we're doing. We rarely get hecklers or CND protesters in the audience. It only happened to me once and I didn't have to do anything. He was just quietly escorted outside and I got on with it."

The lectures follow a fairly standard formula and it is quite usual for a new Team member to find he is giving a talk about the Red Arrows and their history, without actually having flown in a full practice display, let alone at an air show. The pilots will show a set of slides, tell the story of the Red Arrows and what the job entails and explain the role of the Team. Most of the lectures are in Lincolnshire as the Team try to stay within a thirty or forty mile radius of Scampton. They do sometimes go further afield but an overnight stay can interrupt their training programme.

Every year the Team are inundated with requests from the media for facilities to visit the Team, interview them, watch them fly and even go up with them. It is this last request that can cause problems. In the old days the Team took a lot of press writers and photographers for rides and many of them were able to experience a full display practice. Nowadays, permission to fly in practice displays is far harder to get: Nigel Mansell, who was to write an article for the next season's brochure, was one of the few people who did so in 1986. Unlike many civilians – and perhaps because he was used to helmets, masks, high speed and close formation – he really enjoyed his day and was quite happy pulling *g* and seeing the world turn upside down.

Anybody who is flying with the Team will be kitted-up with a helmet, flying gloves, socks, a fireproof flying suit and anti-*g* suit in the Flying Clothing Room. They will be given the seat lecture, to ensure that they know how to eject in an emergency, and told how to arm the seat by removing the pins – they will also be given a sick bag and reminded that if things get too difficult, the ground crew would prefer it if the bag rather than the cockpit was used. Clearing up the mess left by an unhappy civilian is not a favourite task – an RAF visitor flying with the Team is expected to do it himself.

Nearly everyone who gets a ride in the back of a Hawk does feel a little strange in such an alien environment. Annual flights to the sun in a Boeing 737 do not prepare you for a trip with the Red Arrows! Even getting in is tricky; more like climbing into a very high racing car than settling into an airline seat.

Once you are sitting down, the ground crew will help do up the straps and ensure that the radio, oxygen and anti-*g* suit is plugged into the aeroplane. As the canopy comes down you realise how small the cockpit is – although people who flew in the Team before 1980 always say that the Gnat was the aeroplane which really felt as if it were being strapped on to your back. Before you start taxying, the pilot will tell you to remove the pins to arm the ejection system and put them into their special holes – and the ground crew will check that is done before allowing the jet to go.

The back seat in a Hawk is very high and gives a wonderful view over the pilot's head, and as the Hawk gathers speed along the runway apprehension disappears and fatalism takes over. The acceleration is so smooth and swift that in seconds the aeroplane leaps off the runway and you are in the air, banking away from the airfield. Before your stomach has come up to join you, the land has dropped away and you are part of another world. You skip along the top of the clouds with a freedom that does not exist on the ground. Even gravity has to bow to the demands of the little jet. A rash passenger who wants to experience some of the aerobatic manoeuvres that the Red Arrows perform throughout their eighteen-minute show will also experience the effect of pulling *g*. As the aeroplane loops, your body is subjected to extra *g* forces, making it feel several times heavier than normal, and the anti-*g* suit inflates, squeezing your legs and abdomen and ensuring that you don't faint as blood tries to drain from your head.

You know the theory of how it works. In practice, and for a civilian, the squeeze is quite comforting. It feels as if something is on your side. You are, however, not prepared for the fact that the suit seems to inflate to the size of a barrage balloon. You feel like the heaviest sack of potatoes in the world, every part of your body seems intent on pressing through the bottom of the aeroplane, and your arms become immovable lead weights. The pilot who suggested that his passenger give a thumbs down sign, which he would see in his mirror, if he had had enough, had clearly forgotten his first flight and the feeling of total leaden immobility induced by pulling *g* when you are not used to it. As you go over the top of the loop, the *g* fades and you begin to look backwards, waiting for the horizon to appear behind your head. There is a wonderful sensation of floating for a moment – before the *g* returns on the way down.

For most people flying in a fast jet for the first time, there is always the awful dilemma. They want to experience the loops and rolls that are bread and butter to the Team, but few of them can do so without feeling ill. Most civilians are unused to wearing a helmet and tight rubber oxygen mask,

and for many people it is this, as much as the flight itself, which makes them sick.

Many passengers hang on as long as they can before admitting defeat and suggesting that straight and level might be a good way to fly – and the few that are sick usually manage to remember the advice of the ground crew. There are a few passengers, however, whose flights are remembered long after they are on the ground.

One journalist, who was researching an article for his magazine about the joys of flying with a Red Arrow, is probably still recovering from the experience. One of the Team took him up and showed him, as requested, everything the Team did during a display – and more! He survived for a while but then his body decided it had had enough.

The pilot says that every time he asked if his passenger was all right, he replied with something like "yes". It was probably "yerrrch" as he retched yet again into the bag! The journalist's flight and the fact that he spent several hours prostrate in the Crew Room, groaning occasionally as someone enquired politely after his health, before he recovered sufficiently for the long car journey home (fast asleep as a passenger), has gone down in Red Arrows legend. For some time afterwards every prospective passenger was regaled with the story of this hapless journalist's experience and after their own, far less demanding flights, most new passengers realise that it is simply a case of "there but for the grace of God . . ."

Over the years many magazines have written

Left: Down the runway in Big Seven formation on a stormy day to produce an unusual picture for the Illustrated London News

Above: Squadron Leader Richard Thomas signing autographs for ATC cadets at Biggin Hill

pieces about the Red Arrows. Profiles of the pilots, how they work, their home life and how it is affected, have all been covered – and each article has given another opportunity for pictures of the aeroplanes. In the early 1970s the photographer, Richard Cooke, invented the technique for taking rear-facing pictures using a camera mounted underneath a Gnat – flying only a few feet in front of the formation. This had never been attempted before, and had it not been for the Red Arrows' sympathetic attitude to innovation in photography, exciting head-on pictures of aircraft might never have been seen.

Every year the Team get dozens of requests for facilities and flights. "It does take up a lot of time," says Richard Thomas. "I have to keep track of the number of flying hours we dedicate to photography and film. We keep it to an absolute minimum and try and do some of it during normal practices and not mount specific sorties. Obviously publicity is an important side of our job but we are busy training so we have to try and reduce the amount of time we spend flying photographic sorties."

Television companies and radio stations are also constant visitors during the year. They interview pilots, film displays and often include pieces about new Team members and their training. Programmes like Blue Peter have sent their reporters up with the Team, and every other year the Red Arrows are featured as part of the BBC's coverage of Farnborough. One year they superimposed head shots of each pilot, saying a few words to introduce himself, over the film of the display. The one who gave his position, saying it was where the smooth pilots flew, never lived it down – especially as he was also the one who had flown the unhappy journalist.

For most of the public their best chance of seeing the Red Arrows pilots in person is at an air show. "It's a funny job," says Tony Lunnon-Wood. "You go from relative obscurity and then overnight everyone is asking for your autograph. And yet no individual on the Team is really a celebrity – the celebrity is 'The Red Arrows' as a complete unit, the nine red jets. Most people don't

think of us as individuals, but as soon as you get into that jet, or are wearing a red flying suit, suddenly you are special.

"And then in three years you'll be a nothing again, just another bimbo in a green flying suit. You don't have a gradual build up; it is suddenly there and then it is suddenly gone. In the beginning you are quite embarrassed but it is amazing how quickly you get into the groove. You do get a buzz from it when you first start but you have to be careful. You must never get caught in the crowd after a show if you are trying to get to a bus or something. If you do, you can never get away. Then you feel terrible because you have got a queue of kids lined up and you have to say 'I've got to go now' and they think you're a really nasty piece of work, despite the fact that you have probably signed fifty brochures already. You are better off sometimes being totally selfish and going nowhere near the crowd. That way nobody gets an autograph and nobody gets disappointed.

"If there are Service families or if there is a small crowd, you will always go over, particularly if there are some little kids who want to see the aeroplanes. I really enjoy that. After all, the autographs and talking to people are part of the job – and it only lasts three years."

Every year when the pilots are allocated their secondary duties or areas of additional responsibility, two very important jobs always fall to two of the new pilots. One of them is in charge of answering all the letters and requests for posters and information that arrive every week at the station.

Most of the requests are quite straightforward and the Team Manager's staff will help during the season when the pilots are particularly busy, but the people who ask for the Team to do a fly-past for a child's birthday or over a village fête have to receive a polite refusal. Many people write regularly and feel they know the Team – it does not seem to matter that three of the pilots change each year – one fan even moved house from Kemble to Lincolnshire when he heard that the Team were going. Some keen Red Arrows followers send the pilots little presents, but unfortunately the one who sent them a packet of cigarettes failed to address the envelope correctly. The reception desk thought it looked suspicious, the bomb disposal boys were called in and the cigarettes were blown up.

The other first-year pilot looks after "on the road" publicity. He is the man who must be able to produce brochures and stickers on request; and it is his job to ensure that when the Team Leader makes a speech or accepts a gift, he has a framed picture or plaque to give in return.

Pete Collins' first season was in 1986. He was chosen to look after the on the road publicity that year and he didn't always enjoy it: "You have to carry around boxes of brochures and posters and they weigh a ton. People would ask for them in the most obscure places and at the most ridiculous times. I would be standing there with a drink at some reception and they would suddenly come up and ask 'Have you got a signed poster?' I don't know if they thought I had a body bag or something.

"The main thing, though, is to make sure that you have the right things with you if you are going to a reception and the boss needs pictures or things to present. One of the problems is that we land first and may have transport laid on to take us across the airfield. The Hercules, carrying all the publicity material and framed prints, may not arrive until a couple of hours later, after I've gone. Once when I did collect the pictures from the Hercules, I found that the glass in one of the frames had smashed. The chap that picture was for had to make do with a little wooden plaque for his office wall – he looked rather disappointed when everyone else received large signed and framed photographs."

At most of the major air shows a small red caravan can be found amongst the stalls selling souvenirs and hamburgers. This is the Red Arrows Charity Caravan and is run by the "Friends of the Red Arrows". They sell official souvenirs of the Team and the profit they make goes to the RAF Benevolent Fund and other charities. The caravan was first used in 1980 when the Red Arrows were based at Kemble in Gloucestershire.

Wing Commander Brian Hoskins was the Team Leader at that time: "When the weather started to improve in February and March, the lay-by at the end of the runway at Kemble was always jammed with parked cars as people stopped to watch us practise. During the winter it is very much part of the job to both go out and lecture and to accept visitors at the squadron, and we had felt for some time that we ought to do something for all the people watching, especially as many of them were regulars. The pilots couldn't do it as we had to de-brief and watch the video as soon as we landed, but we discussed it with our AOC (Air Officer Commanding) at the time and he thought that some of the wives might like to go over. I spoke to Lizzie, my wife, and she and some of the others decided to take a caravan, park it in the lay-by and sell tea, coffee, soft drinks and a few souvenirs. Everyone who bought anything got a publicity leaflet about the Team and the Benevolent Fund tin was there on the counter for people to put their loose change in. The aims were to make it possible for people to find out more about the Team and to let the Benevolent Fund benefit at the same time.

"Brian Jones and his family became part of it very quickly and they were always willing to lend a hand. When the time came for us to move on, it was unanimously decided that if the Jones' wanted to take over the caravan, then they should."

Brian and Vikki Jones and their two sons live only half a mile away from Kemble. They had been interested in the Red Arrows for some years and when Lizzie Hoskins moved away they were very happy to run the caravan for the Team.

"In 1982 we decided to take the caravan to some air displays," says Brian Jones. "We didn't make much money but we had a marvellous time. In the early days all the money we made went to the Red Arrows and they distributed it to charity, but when John Blackwell was Leader he decided that the Team Fund couldn't handle it, and so we paid it direct to whichever charity we wanted. Most of it went to the RAF Benevolent Fund and when an air show was supporting a particular charity, we would make a donation to them. Since we've

Overleaf: A picture taken for the BBC Television series *The Moment of Truth* which reached an audience of over eight million people

started we have made over £20,000."

At the beginning, the Friends of the Red Arrows didn't exist. There had been an abortive attempt in 1981 to run a fan club, but the company involved had eventually gone bankrupt. Brian Jones was keen to start some kind of association himself. "I left it a couple of years and then in 1983 I wrote to John Blackwell, the Leader, asking if we could do it ourselves. We decided to steer clear of the name fan club and called ourselves the Friends of the Red Arrows. Friends enrol from 1st May and we now end up with about 600 members each year. We have members ranging in age from two to ninety-two and they each get four newsletters a year. Some people write to us, or to the Team and we hand out application forms at air shows. We don't advertise because we couldn't really cope with a rush of eight or ten thousand members and this way we do get people who are really interested."

It was a very sad day for Brian Jones when the Team left Kemble in 1983. "I used to get great pleasure out of being able to take people over to meet the Team and of course I used to be able to watch them practise day after day. Counting the practices, I've probably seen more displays than anyone else in the country – we could see them from our back garden. Now our main job, as well as running the Friends is to take the charity caravan to as many air shows as possible. We are able to keep people in touch with the Team while raising money for Service charities."

For some people, the Red Arrows are their abiding passion and they follow them avidly around the country. Carole Eastwood first became interested in aerobatic teams when her father took her to watch the Black Arrows, the famous team of black Hunters, when she was five. She went to air shows whenever she could and then, when the Red Arrows were formed in 1965, she became one of their most ardent followers. She didn't hear about the Friends until 1985 but now helps on the caravan as often as she can.

"I'm not really interested in the rest of the air show," she says. "Nothing compares with the Red Arrows. You can't beat them, the feeling of excitement when they come over for the beginning of the display. I never ever get tired of watching them. There isn't a room in my house that hasn't got a Red Arrows picture in it. My husband is in the navy and he is away a lot so he is pleased I have an interest.

"I really enjoy helping on the caravan. It became official at the beginning of 1986 and everything we sell is the genuine article. There are a lot of other people making themselves rich at air shows, but we sell exactly the same things as are sold in the Red Arrows' shop at Scampton and all the profit goes to the RAF Benevolent Fund and the Red Arrows Trust."

Air Commodore Blackley was the Commandant of Central Flying School in 1986 and the aerobatic Team were under his command. "Nothing in the Services goes on for ever and the Red Arrows are re-examined regularly at the Ministry of Defence. It's a very expensive item and costs the tax-payer a lot of money, so you have got to look at it and see if you are getting your money's worth. They have been reviewed regularly ever since they started twenty-one years ago and the conclusion has always been the same – they are such good ambassadors and good value, not only for the Royal Air Force but for Britain, that they should continue – and I think they will go on for many years.

"I think they were shown at their best on the Indonesian tour. None of the countries in the Far East had seen anything like it and they were all very enthusiastic. In Jakarta the airfield was overrun with people and there seemed to be as many people outside the perimeter fence as there were inside.

"The crowds varied on the way back to England, depending on whether countries ran the display as an open day for the public or not. But there were always many senior diplomatic representatives and government ministers watching, and everyone was very impressed with the performances of both the aeroplanes and the RAF personnel; both pilots and ground crew.

"Some organisers were worried that it would

cause chaos if they advertised the Red Arrows too widely. The Team gave one display at Bangkok International Airport, and the authorities simply closed the airport down for half an hour. That was quite a feat in itself and they said that if they had announced it in advance, the roads out of Bangkok would have been jammed for hours and would have stopped passengers getting to and from the airport. They invited several government ministers, chiefs of staff and many from the diplomatic corps but didn't announce it publicly until a couple of hours before the display was due to start. There was still quite a big crowd as many people rushed to the airport as soon as they heard.

"Many of the countries were worried about security before the Team arrived so they didn't get a lot of publicity before they went. Once they had displayed they got very good coverage in all the local papers and were the first item on the national television news in several countries. I must admit, I was very disappointed that we didn't get a bit more publicity when we returned to the UK. It *had* been a unique and tremendously successful tour."

Squadron Leader Tim Miller, looking forward to being the Red Arrows Team Leader for the 1988 season, shares the Air Commodore's disappointment. "I think the public relations side of the job is incredibly important, but I think it is also the side of the job where they get the least support. I am sure we could use the Red Arrows more effectively, not just for the RAF but for British industry. It has been done sometimes.

"We went out to the United States ostensibly to celebrate the bi-centenary of manned flight, but it was also a big sales push for the Hawk. When we came back they had a full order book. I'm not claiming that it was simply because of the Red Arrows that the Americans bought the Hawk, but I'm sure it helped. You get an amazing feedback abroad, especially where we haven't been seen before. People, especially ex-patriots, come up and say the Team is the best thing to come out of Britain. It sounds a wild statement but they believe it.

"It must be possible to use the Team better. Obviously we can't get involved in letting companies use them simply for their own commercial gain, but we do live in a commercial world and we could help industries with whom we are already involved. We don't get the media coverage we should either. I think we really should have a professional PR officer, one who really knows the business and who could contact all the local media when we are due to display.

"The PR side of the job does seem to happen by accident. I don't think for one moment that I will be able to change anything, but when I join that is one aspect of the Team that I'd like to try and improve. The Red Arrows really are good news for Britain and the Royal Air Force and we should make the most of them."

"We all call them the Red Arrows," says Air Commodore Blackley, "but their proper name is the Royal Air Force Aerobatic Team, and that is what is written on their crest. They are very much a flagship for the Service and these days it is particularly important to have something like that. Twenty years ago there were many more air displays and more aerobatic teams but nowadays we have to work squadrons so hard that there isn't the money or the time for them to give displays as well. To achieve the sort of level and ability we require from the Red Arrows, they have to do it full time. If you put all your efforts into one thing, you can be sure you will impress and be very good."

The Red Arrows *are* very good, but air-show crowds are likely to be much more effusive in their praise. "Brilliant" is an adjective often used about the Team – its French translation *éclat* has been adopted as their motto and appears on their crest.

Brian Nice, who flew in the first Team in 1965, says: "I really do believe we were the best – I think they are the best in the world now. No question. Nobody can touch the Red Arrows. Not many teams fly nine and nobody flies nine like these guys. Nobody does the rolls, loops and formation changes like these guys do. The other teams don't have the flair and they don't have the innovation. They are the ultimate; we'll not see better in our lifetime."

Overleaf: Smoke billows out behind the Hawks as they loop and roll during a five-four split

The Red Arrows 1965–1987

1965

Leader Flt. Lt. L. Jones
2 Flt. Lt. B. A. Nice
3 Flt. Lt. R. G. Hanna
4 Flt. Lt. G. L. Ranscombe
5 Fg. Off. P. G. Hay
6 Flt. Lt. R. E. W. Loverseed
7 Flt. Lt. H. J. D. Prince
8 Flt. Lt. E. C. F. Tilsley
Manager Sqn. Ldr. R. E. Storer
Engineers Fg. Off. Harrow
　　　　　Fg. Off. Whitby

1966

Leader Sqn. Ldr. R. G. Hanna
2 Flt. Lt. D. A. Bell
3 Flt. Lt. R. W. Langworthy
4 Flt. Lt. P. R. Evans
5 Flt. Lt. R. Booth
6 Flt. Lt. H. J. D. Prince
7 Flt. Lt. T. J. G. Nelson
8 Flt. Lt. F. J. Hoare
9 Flt. Lt. D. McGregor
Manager Sqn. Ldr. R. E. Storer
Engineers Fg. Off. Harrow
　　　　　Fg. Off. Whitby

1967

Leader Sqn. Ldr. R. G. Hanna
2 Flt. Lt. D. A. Bell
3 Flt. Lt. F. J. Hoare
4 Flt. Lt. P. R. Evans
5 Flt. Lt. R. Booth
6 Flt. Lt. H. J. D. Prince
7 Flt. Lt. E. E. Jones
Manager Flt. Lt. L. G. Wilcox
Engineer Fg. Off. D. Whitby
Adjutant Flt. Lt. R. Dench

1968

Leader Sqn. Ldr. R. G. Hanna
2 Flt. Lt. D. A. Bell
3 Flt. Lt. D. A. Smith
4 Flt. Lt. P. R. Evans
5 Flt. Lt. F. J. Hoare
6 Flt. Lt. R. Booth
7 Flt. Lt. J. T. Kingsley
8 Flt. Lt. I. C. H. Dick
9 Flt. Lt. R. B. Duckett
Manager Sqn. Ldr. L. G. Wilcox
Engineer Fg. Off. D. Whitby
Adjutant Flt. Lt. R. Dench

1969

Leader Sqn. Ldr. R. G. Hanna
2 Flt. Lt. P. R. Evans
3 Flt. Lt. D. A. Smith
4 Flt. Lt. R. B. Duckett
5 Flt. Lt. E. R. Perreux
6 Flt. Lt. J. T. Kingsley
7 Flt. Lt. I. C. H. Dick
8 Flt. Lt. J. D. Rust
9 Sqn. Ldr. R. P. Dunn
Manager Flt. Lt. P. MackIntosh
Engineer Fg. Off. G. E. White
Adjutant Flt. Lt. R. Dench

1970

Leader Sqn. Ldr. D. Hazell
2 Flt. Lt. E. R. Perreux
3 Flt. Lt. D. A. Smith
4 Flt. Lt. J. D. Rust
5 Flt. Lt. J. Haddock
6 Flt. Lt. I. C. H. Dick
7 Flt. Lt. R. B. Duckett
8 Flt. Lt. D. S. B. Marr
9 Flt. Lt. R. E. W. Loverseed
Manager Flt. Lt. P. MackIntosh
Engineer Flt. Lt. G. E. White
Adjutant W.O. L. Ludlow

1971

Leader Sqn. Ldr. R. E. W. Loverseed
2 Sqn. Ldr. D. S. B. Marr
3 Flt. Lt. A. C. East
4 Flt. Lt. W. B. Aspinall
5 Flt. Lt. P. J. J. Day
6 Flt. Lt. C. F. Roberts
7 Flt. Lt. R. E. Somerville
Manager Flt. Lt. K. J. Tait
Engineer Flt. Lt. G. E. White
Adjutant W.O. L. Ludlow

1972

Leader Sqn. Ldr. I. C. H. Dick
2 Flt. Lt. W. B. Aspinall
3 Flt. Lt. A. C. East
4 Flt. Lt. R. E. Somerville
5 Flt. Lt. K. J. Tait
6 Flt. Lt. P. J. J. Day
7 Flt. Lt. D. Binnie
8 Flt. Lt. E. E. G. Girdler
9 Flt. Lt. C. F. Roberts
Manager Flt. Lt. B. Donnelly
Engineer Flt. Lt. I. Brackenbury
Adjutant W.O. S. Wild

1973

Leader Sqn. Ldr. I. C. H. Dick
2 Sqn. Ldr. W. B. Aspinall
3 Flt. Lt. B. Donnelly
4 Flt. Lt. E. E. G. Girdler
5 Flt. Lt. K. J. Tait
6 Flt. Lt. D. Binnie
7 Sqn. Ldr. R. E. Somerville
8 Flt. Lt. D. J. Sheen
9 Flt. Lt. P. J. J. Day
Manager Flt. Lt. R. M. Joy
Engineer Flt. Lt. I. Brackenbury
Adjutant W.O. H. E. D. Rundstrom

1974

Leader Sqn. Ldr. I. C. H. Dick
2 Flt. Lt. K. J. Tait
3 Flt. Lt. B. Donnelly
4 Flt. Lt. E. E. G. Girdler
5 Flt. Lt. C. M. Phillips
6 Flt. Lt. D. Binnie
7 Sqn. Ldr. R. E. Somerville
8 Flt. Lt. D. J. Sheen
9 Flt. Lt. R. Eccles
Manager Flt. Lt. R. M. Joy
Engineer Flt. Lt. I. Brackenbury
Adjutant W.O. H. E. D. Rundstrom

1975

Leader Sqn. Ldr. R. B. Duckett
2 Flt. Lt. M. J. Phillips
3 Flt. Lt. B. Donnelly
4 Flt. Lt. R. Eccles
5 Flt. Lt. J. Blackwell
6 Flt. Lt. D. J. Sheen
7 Sqn. Ldr. B. R. Hoskins
8 Flt. Lt. M. Cornwell
9 Flt. Lt. R. S. Barber
Manager Sqn. Ldr. A. L. Wall
Engineer Flt. Lt. A. Hunt
Adjutant W.O. H. E. D. Rundstrom

1976

Leader Sqn. Ldr. R. B. Duckett
2 Flt. Lt. M. J. Phillips
3 Flt. Lt. R. Eccles
4 Flt. Lt. D. R. Carvell
5 Flt. Lt. R. S. Barber
6 Sqn. Ldr. B. R. Hoskins
7 Flt. Lt. M. Cornwell
8 Flt. Lt. M. T. Curley
9 Flt. Lt. N. S. Champness
Manager Sqn. Ldr. A. L. Wall
Engineer Flt. Lt. A. Hunt
Adjutant W.O. H. G. Thorne

1977

Leader Sqn. Ldr. F. J. Hoare
2 Flt. Lt. D. R. Carvell
3 Flt. Lt. R. S. Barber
4 Flt. Lt. M. J. Phillips
5 Flt. Lt. N. S. Champness
6 Flt. Lt. M. Cornwell
7 Flt. Lt. M. T. Curley
8 Flt. Lt. R. M. Thomas
9 Flt. Lt. M. B. Stoner
Manager Flt. Lt. M. B. Whitehouse
Engineer Flt. Lt. A. Hunt
Adjutant W.O. H. G. Thorne

1978

Leader Sqn. Ldr. F. J. Hoare
2 Flt. Lt. D. R. Carvell
3 Flt. Lt. M. B. Stoner
4 Flt. Lt. M. J. Phillips
5 Flt. Lt. L. A. Grose
6 Flt. Lt. M. T. Curley
7 Flt. Lt. R. M. Thomas
8 Flt. Lt. S. R. Johnson
9 Flt. Lt. B. C. Scott
Manager Sqn. Ldr. M. B. Whitehouse
Engineer Flt. Lt. R. A Lewis
Adjutant W.O. H. G. Thorne

1979

Leader Sqn. Ldr. B. R. Hoskins
2 Flt. Lt. M. T. Curley
3 Flt. Lt. B. C. Scott
4 Flt. Lt. M. D. Howell
5 Flt. Lt. M. B. Stoner
6 Flt. Lt. R. M. Thomas
7 Sqn. Ldr. S. R. Johnson
8 Flt. Lt. N. J. Wharton
9 Flt. Lt. W. Ward
Manager Sqn. Ldr. R. Thilthorpe
Engineer Flt. Lt. R. A. Lewis
Adjutant W.O. H. G. Thorne

1980

Leader Sqn. Ldr. B. R. Hoskins
2 Flt. Lt. M. D. Howell
3 Flt. Lt. W. Ward
4 Flt. Lt. N. J. Wharton
5 Flt. Lt. B. C. Scott
6 Flt. Lt. R. M. Thomas
7 Sqn. Ldr. S. R. Johnson
8 Flt. Lt. B. S. Walters
9 Flt. Lt. T. R. Watts
Manager Sqn. Ldr. R. Thilthorpe
Engineer Flt. Lt. R. A. Lewis
Adjutant W.O. H. G. Thorne

1981

Leader Sqn. Ldr. B. R. Hoskins
2 Flt. Lt. B. S. Walters
3 Flt. Lt. W. Ward
4 Flt. Lt. M. H. deCourcier
5 Flt. Lt. N. J. Wharton
6 Sqn. Ldr. S. R. Johnson
7 Flt. Lt. T. R. Watts
8 Flt. Lt. I. J. Huzzard
9 Flt. Lt. J. R. Myers
Manager Sqn. Ldr. R. Thilthorpe
Engineer Flt. Lt. G. M. Nisbet
Adjutant W.O. H. G. Thorne

1982

Leader Sqn. Ldr. J. Blackwell
2 Flt. Lt. B. S. Walters
3 Flt. Lt. J. R. Myers
4 Flt. Lt. I. J. Huzzard
5 Flt. Lt. W. Ward
6 Flt. Lt. T. R. Watts
7 Flt. Lt. M. H. deCourcier
8 Flt. Lt. T. W. L. Miller
9 Flt. Lt. P. A. Tolman
Manager Sqn. Ldr. R. Thilthorpe
Engineer Flt. Lt. G. M. Nisbet
Adjutant W.O. H. G. Thorne

1983

Leader Sqn. Ldr. J. Blackwell
2 Sqn. Ldr. I. J. Huzzard
3 Flt. Lt. J. R. Myers
4 Flt. Lt. T. W. L. Miller
5 Sqn. Ldr. E. H. Ball
6 Flt. Lt. M. H. deCourcier
7 Flt. Lt. P. A. Tolman
8 Flt. Lt. S. H. Bedford
9 Flt. Lt. C. A. R. Hirst
Manager Sqn. Ldr. J. E. Steenson
Engineer Flt. Lt. M. E. J. Render
Adjutant W.O. H. G. Thorne

1984

Leader Sqn. Ldr. J. Blackwell
2 Flt. Lt. S. H. Bedford
3 Flt. Lt. G. I. Hannam
4 Sqn. Ldr. T. W. L. Miller
5 Sqn. Ldr. E. H. Ball
6 Flt. Lt. P. A. Tolman
7 Flt. Lt. A. R. Boyens
8 Flt. Lt. P. D. Lees
9 Flt. Lt. A. K. Lunnon-Wood
Manager Sqn. Ldr. J. E. Steenson
Engineer Flt. Lt. M. E. J. Render
Adjutant W.O. D. H. A. Chubb

1985

Leader Sqn. Ldr. R. M. Thomas
2 Flt. Lt. P. D. Lees
3 Sqn. Ldr. E. H. Ball
4 Flt. Lt. S. H. Bedford
5 Flt. Lt. G. I. Hannam
6 Flt. Lt. A. R. Boyens
7 Flt. Lt. A. K. Lunnon-Wood
8 Flt. Lt. C. D. R. McIlroy
9 Sqn. Ldr. A. B. Chubb
Manager Sqn. Ldr. H. R. Ploszek
Engineer Flt. Lt. M. E. J. Render
Adjutant W.O. D. H. A. Chubb

1986

Leader Sqn. Ldr. R. M. Thomas
2 Flt. Lt. P. D. Lees
3 Sqn. Ldr. A. B. Chubb
4 Flt. Lt. P. J. Collins
5 Sqn. Ldr. G. I. Hannam
6 Flt. Lt. A. K. Lunnon-Wood
7 Flt. Lt. C. D. R. McIlroy
8 Flt. Lt. D. Findlay
9 Flt. Lt. A. P. Thurley
Manager Sqn. Ldr. H. R. Ploszek
Engineer Flt. Lt. J. S. Chantry
Adjutant W.O. D. H. A. Chubb

1987

Leader Sqn. Ldr. R. M. Thomas
2 Sqn. Ldr. P. J. Collins
3 Flt. Lt. M. A. Carter
4 Flt. Lt. M. J. Newbery
5 Sqn. Ldr. A. B. Chubb
6 Flt. Lt. C. D. R. McIlroy
7 Flt. Lt. A. P. Thurley
8 Flt. Lt. J. E. Rands
9 Flt. Lt. G. M. Bancroft-Wilson
Manager Sqn. Ldr. H. R. Ploszek
Engineer Flt. Lt. J. S. Chantry
Adjutant W.O. M. R. J. Fleckney

For those interested in knowing more about the Hawk aircraft flown by the Red Arrows since 1980, British Aerospace PLC have prepared the following technical description.

Previous page: The Synchro Pair practise above the runway at Kemble. Two more Red Arrows' Hawks are taxying beneath them

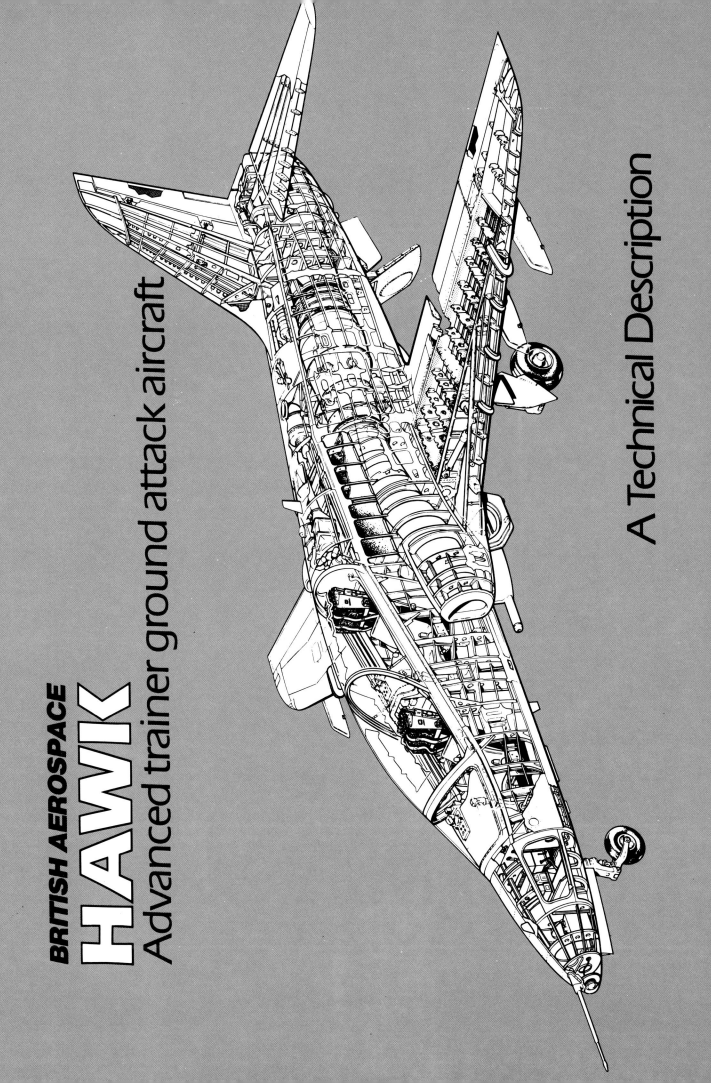

BRITISH AEROSPACE

HAWK
Advanced trainer ground attack aircraft

A Technical Description

Description

The Hawk is a small single-engined two-seat transonic advanced trainer and operational aircraft.

Simplicity of design and manufacture ensures that the Hawk will provide the high utilisation rate and low cost of ownership so essential to meet the exacting demands of cost-effective training and operational use.

The moderately swept wing mounted low on the fuselage is constructed as one complete unit (attached by only 6 bolts making wing removal a speedy and straightforward operation). The wing has slight dihedral and double-slotted flaps. The engine intakes are positioned on the fuselage directly above the wing and slightly forward of the leading edge. The position of the intakes is such that FOD problems are not encountered.

The fin and rudder are positioned well forward in relation to the tailplane and provide excellent spin recovery characteristics by ensuring that the rudder is never completely blanked by the tailplane.

The ailerons and all-moving tailplane are hydraulically operated by a duplicated system. The rudder is manually operated.

The Hawk aircraft is powered by a Rolls-Royce Adour turbofan designed specifically for high reliability in rigorous military service. In addition to the Hawk, the Adour powers the SEPECAT Jaguar and Mitsubishi F-1 and F-2. Adour in-service experience is approaching two million flying hours. Its modular construction reduces spares holdings by 20% and allows greater flexibility of maintenance procedures.

The primary structure of the Hawk is designed for a safe fatigue life of 6 000 hours based on an extremely exacting fatigue spectrum required for the advanced flying training and ground attack roles.

The successful combination of engine and airframe

characteristics provides a rugged, versatile aircraft of very high reliability. Scheduled servicing requirements are minimal and the mean time between engine overhauls is long.

Basic data

Leading particulars

Overall length	38.9ft	11.85m
Span	30.8ft	9.39m
Height	13.1ft	4.0m
Wing area	179.6ft²	16.9m²
Internal usable fuel	375 Imp gal	1 705 litres
Max external usable fuel (drop tanks)	2 x 190 Imp gal	2 x 860 litres
Empty weight (no fuel, no crew)	8 013lb	3 635kg
Max take-off weight	18 390lb	8 340kg
Take-off weight, clean (fuel & two crew)	11 350lb	5 050kg
Engine thrust ISA SLS (Mk 861)	5 700lb	25.4kN
Max normal landing weight	17 000lb	7 650kg

Performance

Max speed (in shallow dive)	Mach 1.2/572kt IAS at 3 000ft	1 060km/h 914m
Max level speed (at sea level)	Mach 0.88/560kt	1 040km/h
Max altitude	50 000ft	15 240m
Max endurance	5½ hours	
Max ferry range	2 200 nm	4 080km
Max external load	6 800lb	3 100kg
Max g	+9.2 and −4.0	
Time to 30 000 ft (clean)	6 minutes	

Major components

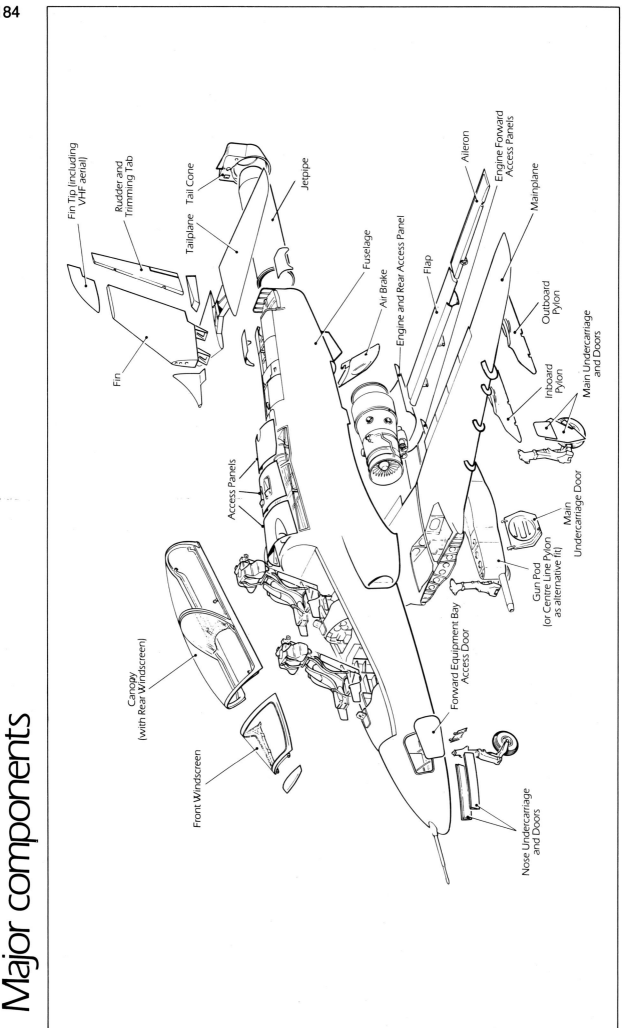

Fin Tip (including VHF aerial)

Rudder and Trimming Tab

Tailplane   Tail Cone

Jetpipe

Fin

Fuselage

Air Brake

Engine and Rear Access Panel

Flap

Aileron

Engine Forward Access Panels

Mainplane

Outboard Pylon

Inboard Pylon

Main Undercarriage and Doors

Access Panels

Main Undercarriage Door

Gun Pod (or Centre Line Pylon as alternative fit)

Canopy (with Rear Windscreen)

Forward Equipment Bay Access Door

Front Windscreen

Nose Undercarriage and Doors

Structure

The Hawk structure consists almost entirely of aluminium alloy sheetwork, extrusions and machined parts, with a relatively small quantity of steel used for highly loaded fittings and a small number of magnesium alloy castings. The aluminium alloys are generally of the copper bearing variety, used either in the naturally or artificially age hardened condition as the loading demands. All structure is assembled with chromated jointing compound or Thiokol tank sealant, and electrolytic corrosion between dissimilar metals is avoided by the use of coatings such as cadmium plate or zinc spray.

Riveting is generally by means of solid aluminium alloy rivets, placed in the softened condition, but where conditions demand, some blind rivets are employed. Bolts are all close tolerance steel bolts to ISO metric standard and are cadmium plated. For general structural work, nuts used are of the self-locking distorted-thread type, but split cotter pins or wire locking is used in flying controls and similar important functions.

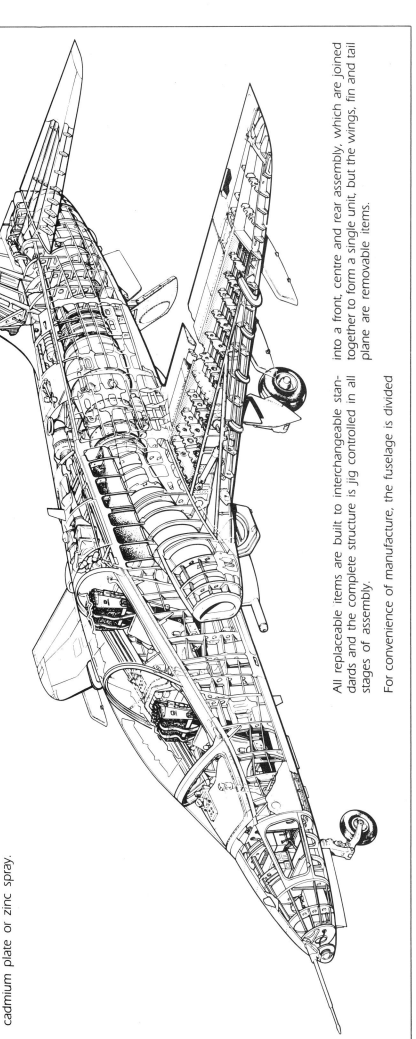

All replaceable items are built to interchangeable standards and the complete structure is jig controlled in all stages of assembly.

For convenience of manufacture, the fuselage is divided into a front, centre and rear assembly, which are joined together to form a single unit, but the wings, fin and tail plane are removable items.

Front cockpit

Considerable attention has been given to human engineering in the design and layout of the spacious cockpits. All instruments and controls are logically grouped together, with the majority placed well ahead and in easy view of the pilot.

Mk 60 front cockpit layout with 5-pylon armament system

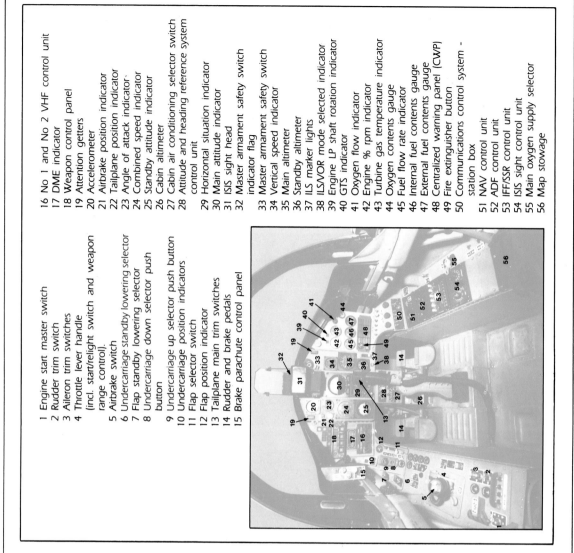

1 Engine start master switch
2 Rudder trim switch
3 Aileron trim switches
4 Throttle lever handle (incl. start/relight switch and weapon range control)
5 Airbrake switch
6 Undercarriage standby lowering selector
7 Flap standby lowering selector
8 Undercarriage down selector push button
9 Undercarriage up selector push button
10 Undercarriage position indicators
11 Flap selector switch
12 Flap position indicator
13 Tailplane main trim switches
14 Rudder and brake pedals
15 Brake parachute control panel

16 No 1 and No 2 VHF control unit
17 DME indicator
18 Weapon control panel
19 Attention getters
20 Accelerometer
21 Airbrake position indicator
22 Tailplane position indicator
23 Angle of attack indicator
24 Combined speed indicator
25 Standby attitude indicator
26 Cabin altimeter
27 Cabin air conditioning selector switch
28 Attitude and heading reference system control unit
29 Horizontal situation indicator
30 Main attitude indicator
31 ISIS sight head
32 Master armament safety switch indicator flag
33 Master armament safety switch
34 Vertical speed indicator
35 Main altimeter
36 Standby altimeter
37 ILS marker lights
38 ILS/VOR mode selected indicator
39 Engine LP shaft rotation indicator
40 GTS indicator
41 Oxygen flow indicator
42 Engine % rpm indicator
43 Turbine gas temperature indicator
44 Oxygen contents gauge
45 Fuel flow rate indicator
46 Internal fuel contents gauge
47 External fuel contents gauge
48 Centralized warning panel (CWP)
49 Fire extinguisher button
50 Communications control system - station box
51 NAV control unit
52 ADF control unit
53 IFF/SSR control unit
54 ISIS sight control unit
55 Main oxygen supply selector
56 Map stowage

Rear cockpit

The majority of non-flying controls are in the front cockpit. However, if a Hawk operator particularly required complete duplication of all controls, the aircraft could be so equipped.

Mk 60 rear cockpit with 5-pylon armament system

1 Engine start master switch
2 Rudder trim switch
3 Aileron trim switch
4 Throttle lever handle (incl. start/relight switches and weapon range control)
5 Airbrake switch
6 Undercarriage standby lowering selector
7 Flap standby lowering selector
8 Undercarriage down selector push button
9 Undercarriage up selector push button and solenoid lock override
10 Undercarriage position indicators
11 Flap selector switch
12 Flap position indicator
13 Tailplane main trim switches
14 Rudders and brake pedals
15 DME indicator
16 Weapon monitor panel
17 Attention getters
18 Accelerometer
19 Airbrake position indicator
20 Tailplane position indicator
21 Angle of attack indicator
22 Combined speed indicator
23 Standby attitude indicator
24 Cabin pressure altimeter
25 Horizontal situation indicator
26 Main attitude indicator
27 ISIS sight head
28 Vertical speed indicator
29 Main altimeter
30 Standby altimeter
31 ILS marker lights
32 ILS/VOR mode selected indicator
33 Engine LP shaft rotation indicator
34 GTS indicator
35 Oxygen flow indicator
36 Engine % rpm indicator
37 Turbine gas temperature indicator
38 Oxygen contents gauge
39 Fuel flow rate indicator
40 Internal fuel contents gauge
41 External fuel contents gauge
42 Centralized warning panel (CWP)
43 Fire extinguisher
44 Communications control system - station box
45 ISIS sight control unit
46 Main oxygen supply selector
47 Map stowage

Flying controls

Mechanical Control Circuit

The input circuit from the conventional control columns and rudder pedals to the tailplane, ailerons and rudder comprises push-pull rods and mechanical links and levers. No control cables are used.

Control rods are generally of aluminium except in the engine bay area where stainless steel is used.

Longitudinal Control

Longitudinal control is by an all-moving tailplane which is powered by a tandem hydraulic servo actuator centrally mounted at the base of the fin.

A mechanical feedback linkage on the ram of the actuator centralizes the servo control valves, following pilot input, when the tailplane reaches the desired position.

The actuator is supplied with the power from the aircraft's two independent hydraulic systems, such that the integrity of one system is not affected by failure of the other. Actuator design is such that interconnection of the two hydraulic systems is not possible.

Control movements are transmitted from the control columns to the powered actuator input lever by push-pull rods. Non-linear gearing is incorporated in the mechanical input circuit to provide the required sensitivity characteristic between control column and tailplane positions.

Artificial feel is provided, to give suitable forces at the control column, from a combination of two sources. A dual gradient spring feel unit provides a force as a function of displacement, and superimposed on this is the contribution from an inertia weight giving a stick force proportional to 'g'.

Trimming is achieved by adjusting the null force position of the spring feel unit by means of a linear electric actuator which is provided with main and standby motors. The motors are prevented from operating simultaneously.

Lateral Control

Lateral control is provided by conventional ailerons, each powered by a tandem hydraulic servo actuator similar in operation to that used for the tailplane control. A bell-crank lever directs movements from the fuselage circuit to the wing port and starboard actuators. Control column movement, relative to aileron deflection, is linear. Artificial feel is provided to give suitable forces at the control column by a spring feel unit. Trim is achieved by adjusting the null force position of the spring feel unit by means of a single motor linear electric actuator.

Directional Control

Directional control is provided by a conventional, operated directly through a series of push-pull ro⟨ ⟩n the rudder pedals. The rudder-to-pedal relationship is linear.

A spring unit is included in the mechanical circuit to provide rudder centring. An electric rotary acutator driving a rudder tab provides trim control. The rudder can be mechanically locked in the neutral position using a cockpit located control for parking in high wind conditions.

Flying Controls

Labels: Rudder, Trim Tab, Tailplane Tandem Jack, Tailplane, Tailplane Non-Linear Gearing, Port Aileron, Aileron Tandem Jack, Idler Levers, Aileron Idler Levers, Tailplane Spring Feel Unit, Tailplane Trim Actuator, Rudder Centring Unit, Starboard Aileron, Aileron Tandem Jack, Aileron Spring Feel Unit, Aileron Trim Actuator, Rear Control Column, Swivel Rod Assembly, Tailplane Circuit, Rudder Circuit, Aileron Circuit, Front Control Column, Rudder Gust Lock, Inertia Weight

NOTE
Port Rudder Pedals
and Control Unit Mountings
Omitted for Clarity

The rudder pedals in each cockpit have adjustable leg reach facility and toe pedals for operation of the independent hydraulic wheelbrakes.

Position Indicators

Tailplane, aileron trim and rudder trim position indicators are provided in each cockpit.

Control Column

The control column handgrip contains switches for the following functions: lateral and longitudinal trim, communications, weapon release, gun trigger and camera recorder. Trim selections made from the rear cockpit will override those from the front cockpit.

Aileron-Powered Flying Control Unit

Each unit (jack) comprises a tandem piston assembly moving within the PCU cylinders. The units are of the moving ram type, i.e. the body of the unit is bolted to a bracket beneath the wing lower surface, whilst the ram eye-end is attached to the aileron. The unit, which employs a form of non-linear gearing and a feedback link to operate the valves, is not adjustable for length, rigging adjustments being effected at the input rod. A hole through the inner end outer levers provides for the use of a rigging tool to neutralize the jack.

Tailplane-Powered Flying Control Unit

The tailplane flying control unit comprises two half bodies bolted together, in which a piston and ram rod assembly reciprocates. The body of the unit is attached by a trunnion fitting to a bracket on the aft face of frame 31, whilst the ram eye-end is secured to a bracket bolted to the top of the tail plane. The unit, which employs an input lever and coupled feed back link to operate the valves, is not adjustable for length. The PCU is controlled by a pair of servo valves which are supplied by two completely independent hydraulic systems as a precaution against failure.

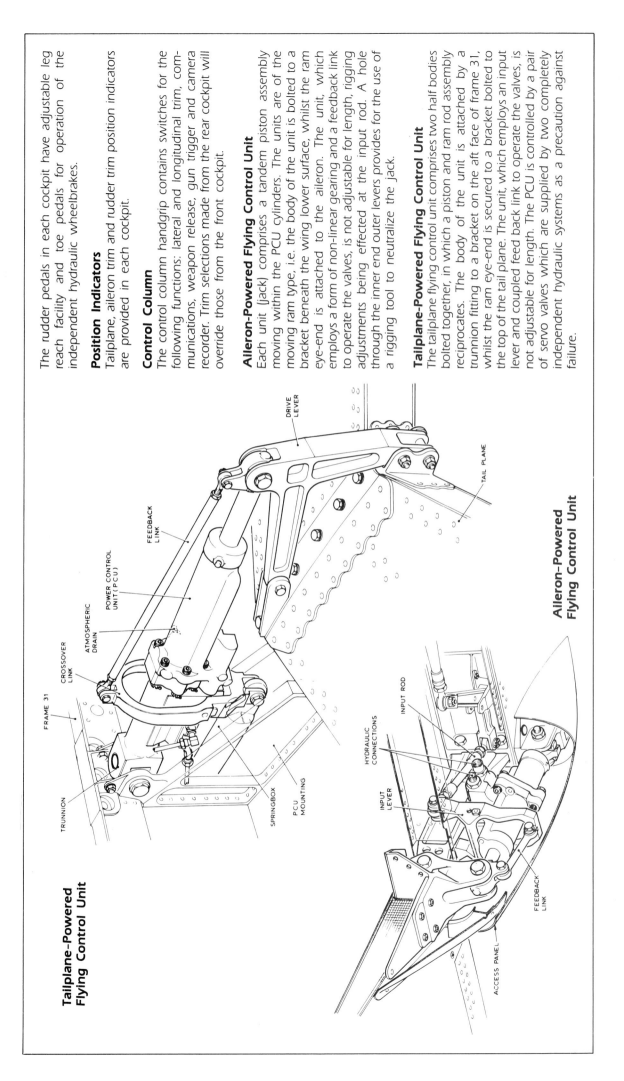

Tailplane-Powered
Flying Control Unit

FRAME 31

TRUNNION

CROSSOVER LINK

ATMOSPHERIC DRAIN

POWER CONTROL UNIT (PCU)

FEEDBACK LINK

DRIVE LEVER

TAIL PLANE

SPRINGBOX

PCU MOUNTING

Aileron-Powered
Flying Control Unit

INPUT ROD

HYDRAULIC CONNECTIONS

INPUT LEVER

FEEDBACK LINK

ACCESS PANEL

Location of equipment

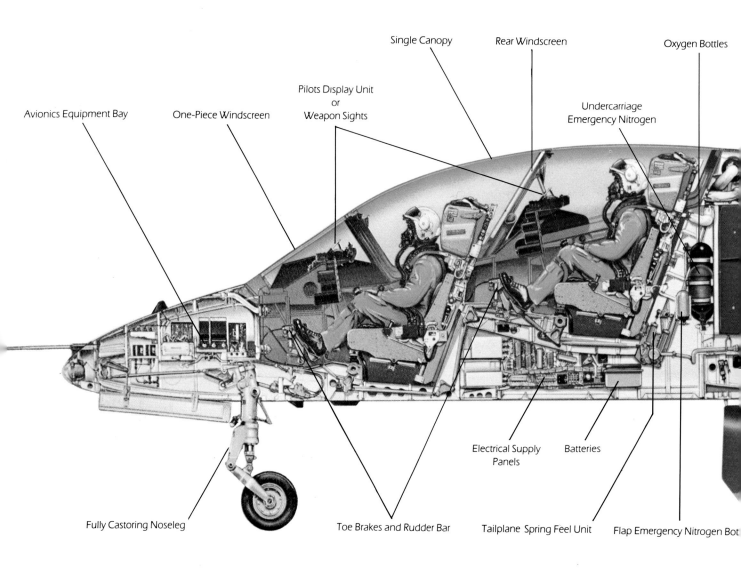

Single Canopy

Rear Windscreen

Oxygen Bottles

Pilots Display Unit
or
Weapon Sights

Avionics Equipment Bay

One-Piece Windscreen

Undercarriage
Emergency Nitrogen

Electrical Supply
Panels

Batteries

Fully Castoring Noseleg

Toe Brakes and Rudder Bar

Tailplane Spring Feel Unit

Flap Emergency Nitrogen Bot

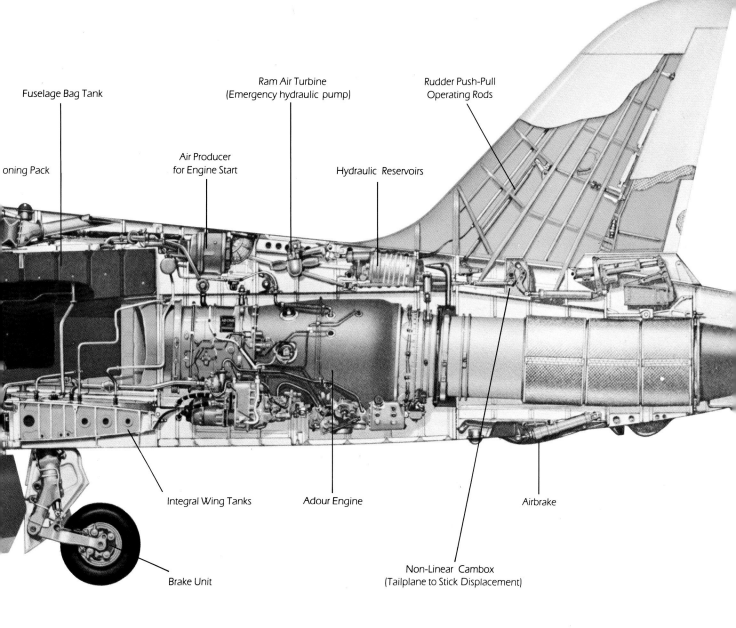

Fuselage Bag Tank

oning Pack

Ram Air Turbine
(Emergency hydraulic pump)

Air Producer
for Engine Start

Rudder Push-Pull
Operating Rods

Hydraulic Reservoirs

Integral Wing Tanks

Adour Engine

Airbrake

Brake Unit

Non-Linear Cambox
(Tailplane to Stick Displacement)

Avionics

A comprehensive range of communications and navigation equipment is available according to customer requirement.

Examples of equipment fit.

	Type Number	Manufacturer
Communication:		
VHF	VHF 20B	Collins
UHF	AN/ARC 159	Collins
UHF/VHF	AN/ARC 182	Collins
Intercom	697 series	Racal Acoustics
Navigation:		
Tacan	AN/ARN 118	Collins
VOR/ILS	VIR 31A	Collins
IFF/SSR	2720	Cossor
Twin Gyro Platform	6000S	Lear Siegler
DME	DME-40	Collins
ADF	51Y-7	Collins
Radar Altimeter	0101 KTX-1	Smiths
Weapon System:		
Gunsight	ISIS D195R Mk 5	Ferranti
Camera Recorder	C121	Ferranti
Weapon Control System	5 Pylon	CDC

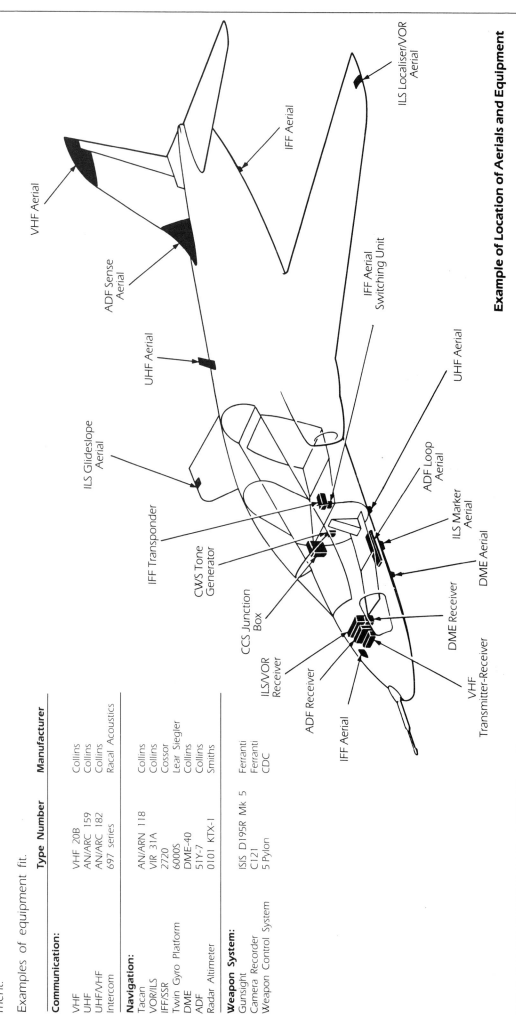

Example of Location of Aerials and Equipment

VHF Aerial

ADF Sense Aerial

UHF Aerial

ILS Glideslope Aerial

IFF Transponder

CWS Tone Generator

CCS Junction Box

ILS/VOR Receiver

ADF Receiver

IFF Aerial

VHF Transmitter-Receiver

DME Receiver

DME Aerial

ILS Marker Aerial

ADF Loop Aerial

UHF Aerial

IFF Aerial Switching Unit

IFF Aerial

ILS Localiser/VOR Aerial

Oxygen system

Main System

A gaseous oxygen system is provided. The gas is stored in two 1 400 litre wire-wound cylinders mounted behind the rear seat frame. From the cylinders, the oxygen flows through a single pressure regulating valve after which the flow is divided between both crew positions. Each pilot is provided with a console-mounted shut-off valve and a demand oxygen regulator installed on the seat section of his personal equipment connector. 'AIRMIX' or '100% OXYGEN' is selected by a sliding lever mounted on the regulator.

Emergency Oxygen

An emergency oxygen cylinder and release mechanism is mounted on the back of each ejection seat. This cylinder has a capacity of 70 litres and the supply is routed through the seat-mounted demand regulator. An 'EMERGENCY OXYGEN' selection automatically ensures a supply of 100% oxygen irrespective of the previous selection.

Duration

Aircrew oxygen gives an approximate duration of 4 hours on 'AIRMIX' continuous and 2½ hours on '100%' continuous for the following flight profile with 2 crew members:

- take-off and climb to 35 000 ft,
- cruise at 35 000 ft,
- descend and land.

Cockpit Indicators

Each pilot has a contents gauge, dolls eye flow indicator and a failure warning light on the central warning panel. This light, marked 'OXY', illuminates when the supply pressure downstream of the isolation valve falls below 45 psi (310 kPa). This pressure is sensed by the low pressure warning switch.

Escape system

The Hawk escape system is composed of the following elements:

● ejection seat
● canopy fracturing system
● command ejection system.

Ejection Seat

Each cockpit is equipped with a fully automatic Martin-Baker Mk 10 series rocket-assisted ejection seat which provides escape facilities at all altitudes and speeds within the flight envelope of the aircraft down to zero height/zero speed.

The seat consists of three principal sub-assemblies:

● ejection gun
● main beams
● seat pan.

Ejection Gun

Ejection of the seat is initiated by a multi-cartridge telescopic gun, composed of an outer tube attached to the airframe which guides the seat clear of the aircraft, an intermediate tube and an inner tube which imparts propulsive forces to the seat. The seat is fixed to the outer tube by a top latch mechanism which is automatically released by the firing of the gun on ejection.

Main beams

Two upright rectangular hollow section main beams slide on guide rails attached to the outer tube of the ejection gun. The beams carry the seat pan, harness reeling mechanism, parachute and drogue container, barostatic time delay mechanism, drogue gun and electric motor for seat pan height adjustment.

Seat Pan

The seat pan is a structural assembly which forms a seating platform and backrest for the crewman and is attached to two tubes mounted on the forward face of

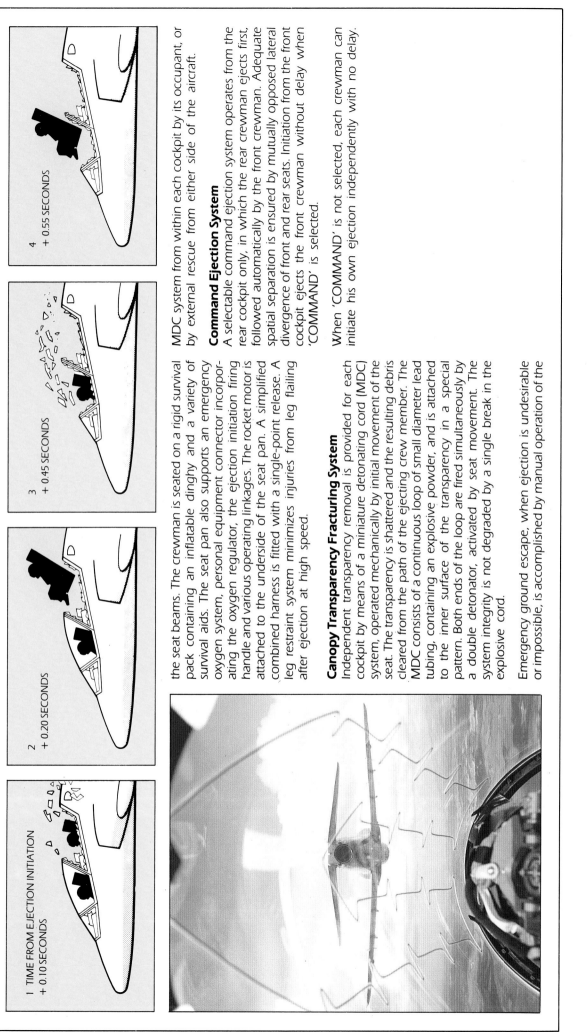

1 TIME FROM EJECTION INITIATION
+ 0.10 SECONDS

2 + 0.20 SECONDS

3 + 0.45 SECONDS

4 + 0.55 SECONDS

the seat beams. The crewman is seated on a rigid survival pack containing an inflatable dinghy and a variety of survival aids. The seat pan also supports an emergency oxygen system, personal equipment connector incorporating the oxygen regulator, the ejection initiation firing handle and various operating linkages. The rocket motor is attached to the underside of the seat pan. A simplified combined harness is fitted with a single-point release. A leg restraint system minimizes injuries from leg flailing after ejection at high speed.

Canopy Transparency Fracturing System

Independent transparency removal is provided for each cockpit by means of a miniature detonating cord (MDC) system, operated mechanically by initial movement of the seat. The transparency is shattered and the resulting debris cleared from the path of the ejecting crew member. The MDC consists of a continuous loop of small diameter lead tubing, containing an explosive powder, and is attached to the inner surface of the transparency in a special pattern. Both ends of the loop are fired simultaneously by a double detonator, activated by seat movement. The system integrity is not degraded by a single break in the explosive cord.

Emergency ground escape, when ejection is undesirable or impossible, is accomplished by manual operation of the

MDC system from within each cockpit by its occupant, or by external rescue from either side of the aircraft.

Command Ejection System

A selectable command ejection system operates from the rear cockpit only, in which the rear crewman ejects first, followed automatically by the front crewman. Adequate spatial separation is ensured by mutually opposed lateral divergence of front and rear seats. Initiation from the front cockpit ejects the front crewman without delay when 'COMMAND' is selected.

When 'COMMAND' is not selected, each crewman can initiate his own ejection independently with no delay.

Advanced trainer/ground attack aircraft

ALL-THROUGH JET TRAINER

From take-off to touchdown, Hawk is responsive, agile, predictable and safe - everything that a trainer should be. It is a pilot's aircraft, allowing the student to confidently progress from basic training to front-line combat missions.

Hawk's easy ground handling, modest 2 000 ft (600m) runway requirement and low take-off and landing speeds are immediately appreciated by the student. Also reassuring are the minimal trim changes as flaps and gear are retracted or extended. Take-off or landing in crosswinds of up to 25 kt poses no problems, with or without external stores.

From basic training, the student remains with the Hawk throughout the training spectrum. The demanding regime of advanced weapon training fully exploits Hawk's ample reserves of power to give sustained high speeds with weapons. Representative combat practice convincingly demonstrates the agility of the Hawk, resulting from its high energy interchange capabilities. Itself fully capable of front-line missions, the Hawk maintains its training efficiency right up to operational conversion.

Superb Handling

Hawk is exceptionally spin-resistant and requires full rudder to initiate and hold a spin, recovering in one turn when the controls are centralized. Stall characteristics are progressive and predictable, with no tendency to depart. Recovery is immediate by releasing back pressure on the stick.

Positive control is maintained throughout the flight envelope up to Mach 1.2 which is achievable and self-limiting in a dive from high altitude.

The Hawk is fully aerobatic - a fact convincingly demonstrated by the RAF Red Arrows display team. The rugged airframe is cleared from +8g to −4g and its

advanced aerodynamics enable a 6g turn at low altitude to be sustained without loss of speed or height. A typical rate of turn at 400 kt (835 km/hr) is 16 degrees per second.

Flying Classroom

With a one-piece canopy, both cockpits offer an almost unrestricted field of vision, and low noise levels permit relaxed communication during all aspects of in-flight training. Roomy cockpits and a logical layout of instruments - including duplicated weapon sights - provide an ideal 'classroom' environment for the student and instructor.

The use of advanced design technology has evolved a compact, efficient aircraft capable of carrying a disposable load which exceeds its empty weight. Hawk's unexcelled flying qualities provide a stable platform for precision delivery of a wide range of ordnance.

The rugged structure capably handles warloads of up to 6 800 lb (3 100 kg) carried beneath the fuselage and at four underwing stores stations.

Uncompromised Performance

Flying characteristics, manoeuvring limits and fatigue endurance are virtually unimpaired when carrying heavy warloads. A load factor of +8g applies with warloads of up to 3 000 lb (1 360 kg) and remains high at +6g with a 5 000 lb (2 270 kg) load.

High Speed, Long Range

High attack speed is vital for survival. Fully loaded with nine 550 lb (250 kg) bombs, Hawk is cleared to 500 kt, even at low level.

Already substantial, the Hawk's radius of action can be significantly extended by fitting external fuel tanks of 130 Imp gal (590 litre) or 190 Imp gal (860 litre) capacity.

Missile Missions

Hawk efficiently performs missile and air defence missions armed with up to four air-to-air missiles and a 30 mm cannon. With two Sidewinder missiles and gunpod, Hawk can reach 30 000 ft altitude in less than eight minutes from brake release. In the same configuration, turn rate is 14 degrees per second at 400 kt.

High manoeuvrability, good climb performance and long endurance, combined with the ability to carry a heavy and varied warload, make the Hawk well suited to tactical offensive support operations.

Armament

Carriage of underwing weapons has little effect on the handling qualities of the Hawk, even with high drag weapons. The wing stations will accept twin-store carriers, allowing a total of nine external stores. For example, nine BR 250 bombs - equivalent of the US Mk 82 550 lb (250 kg) - have been flown satisfactorily at speeds up to 500 knots (M0.85). With a warload of 3 000 lb and 60% fuel remaining (typical over-target condition) an 8g load factor is retained. Above 3 000 lb warload the load factor permitted is reduced to 6g.

It is a measure of the Hawk's advanced design standards that its attack performance carrying large weapon loads is unimpaired in respect of flying qualities, manoeuvring limits, strength and fatigue endurance.

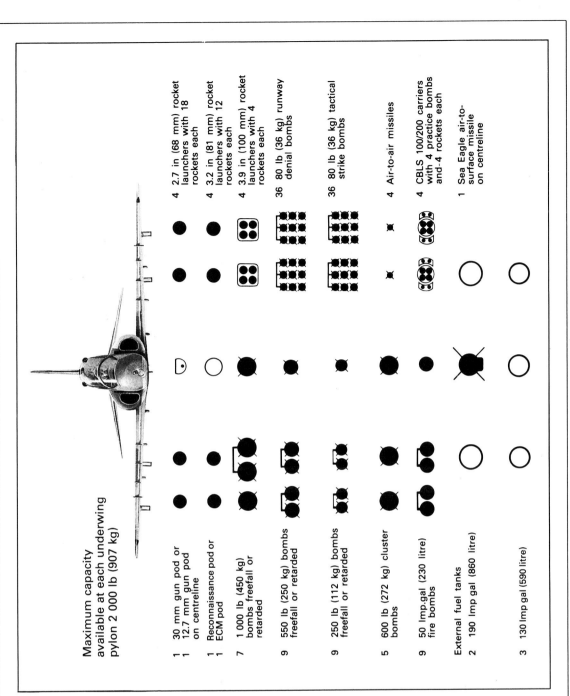

Maximum capacity available at each underwing pylon 2 000 lb (907 kg)

1 30 mm gun pod or
1 12.7 mm gun pod on centreline

1 Reconnaissance pod or
1 ECM pod

7 1 000 lb (450 kg) bombs freefall or retarded

9 550 lb (250 kg) bombs freefall or retarded

9 250 lb (112 kg) bombs freefall or retarded

5 600 lb (272 kg) cluster bombs

9 50 Imp.gal (230 litre) fire bombs

External fuel tanks
2 190 Imp gal (860 litre)

3 130 Imp gal (590 litre)

4 2.7 in (68 mm) rocket launchers with 18 rockets each

4 3.2 in (81 mm) rocket launchers with 12 rockets each

4 3.9 in (100 mm) rocket launchers with 4 rockets each

36 80 lb (36 kg) runway denial bombs

36 80 lb (36 kg) tactical strike bombs

4 Air-to-air missiles

4 CBLS 100/200 carriers with 4 practice bombs and 4 rockets each

1 Sea Eagle air-to-surface missile on centreline

Engine

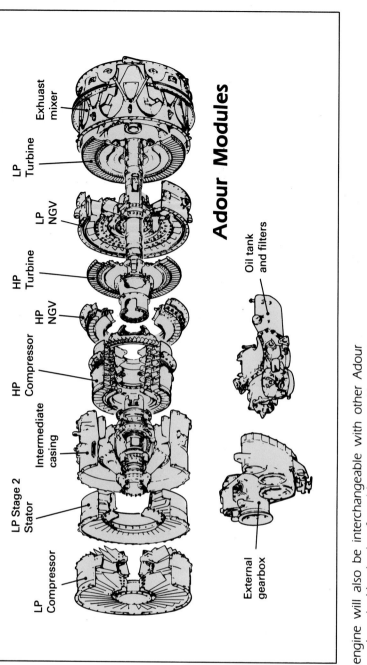

Adour Modules

LP Compressor

LP Stage 2 Stator

Intermediate casing

HP Compressor

HP NGV

HP Turbine

LP NGV

LP Turbine

Exhuast mixer

External gearbox

Oil tank and filters

The Hawk is powered by the Rolls-Royce Turbomeca Adour Mk 861 turbofan. The engine has a bypass ratio of 0.75, and develops a sea-level static thrust of 5 700 lb (25.4 kN) under ISA conditions. The modular construction of the engine minimizes the inventory of complete engines which must he held as spares. All the main rotor modules are pre-balanced to a common standard, enabling these to be exchanged without any need for further balancing.

The low-pressure (LP) system consists of a two-stage compressor driven by a single-stage turbine, supported by three bearings. There are no inlet guide vanes, and the first stage rotor blades are made of titanium with the rest of the LP compressor aerofoils of aluminium alloy.

The high-pressure (HP) system consists of a five-stage titanium-bladed compressor with steel stator vanes driven by a single-stage air-cooled turbine, supported by two bearings. The compressor has no inlet guide vanes and the one bleed valve is used for starting only. There are no variable stator vanes with the LP and HP system. The blades of both HP and LP compressors are low aspect ratio and made of materials selected to give a robust construction with resistance to foreign object damage (FOD).

The combustion system is a single, fully annular chamber with 18 simplex airspray fuel injectors. The bypass airflow is mixed with the hot gas stream in the jet-pipe.

Adour Engine Growth Potential

The Adour engine has considerable growth potential due to its moderate operating temperatures and pressures, and rugged construction.

Rolls-Royce Turboméca are taking advantage of this potential in that the Mk 871 version of the Adour has been launched for development. This engine will produce up to 18% more thrust than the Mk 861, depending on flight conditions, with similar cruise fuel consumption. The

engine will also be interchangeable with other Adour engines in Hawk aircraft, subject to some wiring and instrumentation changes. The Mk 871 engine will still feature state-of-the-art engine technology, leaving scope for even further growth with the use of advanced compressor and turbine technologies in the future.

An integral gas turbine starter, using aircraft fuel, is employed so that the Hawk is independent of external starting aids.

Engine access and removal is through large doors beneath the engine bay.

Rolls-Royce Adour

Hawk development

Since introduction into RAF service in 1976, Hawk has benefited from a continuing programme of product development. Engine thrust growth has been matched by aerodynamic improvement of the rugged airframe to provide enhanced training and operational mission capability. Worldwide sales now exceed 300 aircraft to nine air arms.

Emphasising its design integrity and proven efficiency, Hawk has been selected by the US Navy as the basis for its advanced jet strike training system (STS). Over 300 T-45A Goshawk aircraft are required, fully developed for US Navy carrier training.

Keeping in step with advancing technology, the Hawk 100 two-seat dedicated ground attack aircraft and the Hawk 200 single-seat multi-role attack variant are equipped with state-of-the-art avionics. Each of these major developments combines the Hawk's superior in-flight agility and heavy warload capability with improved navigation and attack accuracy.

A docile, yet challenging trainer - a robust and hard-hitting frontline weapons system, Hawk continues to demonstrate its unique blend of multi-role versatility and cost effectiveness.

Year of entry into service

	75	76	77	78	79	80	81	82	83	84	85	86	87	88	89	90
T Mk 1 Royal Air Force		▲ 176 aircraft														
Mk 50 British Aerospace		▲ 1 demonstrator/development aircraft														
Mk 51 Finland						▲ 50 aircraft										
Mk 52 Kenya						▲ 12 aircraft										
Mk 53 Indonesia						▲ 20 aircraft										
Mk 60 Zimbabwe								▲ 8 aircraft								
Mk 61 Dubai									▲ 8 aircraft							
Mk 63 Abu Dhabi										▲ 16 aircraft						
Mk 64 Kuwait											▲ 12 aircraft					
T-45A US Navy														▲ 302 aircraft		
Hawk 100 Advanced ground attack aircraft												▲				
Hawk 200 Single-seat fighter											▲					
Mk 65 Saudi Arabia													▲ 30 aircraft			
Swiss Military Department															▲ 20 aircraft*	

Total hours flown currently over 500 000

*To be confirmed